Too Soon et pero Too Late

French Grace. American Collapse. Colombian Care.

Hawtorn V. Rabot

Thumb Confessions

Printed in the United States of America.
ISBN: 979-8-9999336-0-7
First Edition

Foreword

This story was written in the middle of another book. Most of it came during two plane rides: one while I was beyond ill, the other while I was recovering. The rest came during one night with a view and two days of recovery. The book took less than three weeks to finish.

Some details, facts, and locations have been altered to protect identities. Certain events were removed, and others were invented. Any resemblance is purely coincidental.

Everything in this memoir reflects events exactly as the narrator experienced them.

Writer's Advisory

This memoir contains descriptions of abuse, grooming, sexual violence, marital conflict, sexual content, and language that may be disturbing for some readers.

This story is recommended for mature readers.

Reader discretion is advised.

Dedication

For the French, Colombian, and Ugandan people who treated me better than family.

For my daughter.

I will always treat you the way the French, Colombian, and Ugandan people always treat me.

I will do even better.

Table of Contents

Episode I: Landing

Chapter A Drop

My dream fractured. My body gasped and swam awake. I half choked. Sweat soaked my sheets. My head spun. I wasn't hungover. My mouth was dry.

I was flying to Bogotá, connecting to Cartagena, and ending in Barranquilla.

I was moving slowly and gingerly, but I moved with purpose.

***

The ride from the small town to the airport was 'quick and angry' through the Andes. The driver was polished; the turns were raw. I didn't want to fall over, vomit foam, or worse. My stomach folded on itself.

I knew my vacation was over, and I needed a medical holiday. Stopping in Bogotá was not a choice. It was a need; I needed help. My head spun the decision for me.

I messaged Ondine that I wasn't doing well. I wanted to stop in Bogotá, get a doctor, and recover. I asked if she could do that. Could she arrange it all the way Isaline would have? The way Isaline would have taken care of me?

She said that would mean no refunds.

I said okay. I understand. If you get travel credits, please give them to Isaline for her trouble.

She said there would be no credits. Do I cancel?

I said yes. If you get credits, or if there are people who need my reservations, please pay it forward.

Ondine, the literal French businesswoman. Isaline would have anticipated it and had a finger on the Enter button, awaiting confirmation. She would have handled it and sent me the confirmation. That is no judgment on you, Ondine. I mean that. But Isaline is the mail carrier who always delivers.

Ondine said the best option was for me to book my own hotel and driver. I texted back   . I needed a decent connection for that.

***

I couldn't get Wi-Fi or reception. My phone rejected every network's security. My body begged it to connect, but the phone had its own mind. My body needed help, and my phone said wait.

I made sure my bags stopped in Bogotá. My Spanish was slow and slurred, and I was forgetting it. The airline attendants didn't speak English, but they confirmed my bags would stop in Bogotá.

***

On the plane, I was sweating and seeing three of everything. One on the left, one on the right, one in the center. Were planes always this hot?

Still, I wrote my review of the company. I aimed for the phone in the center. The phones on the left and right were blurs.

And I kept writing this story.

But I squeezed the phone in case I collapsed.

I *needed* **someone** to get the story *down*.

The air came weakly from the vents. Inside my head, balance and direction leaked.

Thumb. Phone. Body. The need to write.

My feet braced against the floor; my back pressed flat to the chair.

I left the present.

I retreated into my memories.

Part 1 Amazon

I was in before, where it began. But I was still sick on the plane. Still holding on.

At least parts of it started where the air was clear, and the water moved naturally.

Before COVID, my wife and I went to Ecuador. After constant West Coast trips and Europe, it was my turn to pick.

We saw Quito, the cloud forest, and the Amazon. Everything on the trip was beautiful, and I loved it all. Well, almost everything. My wife whined about every inconvenience or ache. Some of my wife's complaints were real. Some were imaginary. Either way, I had to listen. I wasn't paid for my time.

But the quieter the setting and the wilder the nature, the more I could breathe. It sure beat the noise and crowds of Prague and Barcelona.

The Amazon was the greatest, and the rest was a distant second. I loved the rustic lodge in the jungle with mosquito nets. It was stripped of most modern conveniences. On most trips since, I've tried to find something, *anything*, like it.

We were with a friendly German couple and an animated French group. They represented their nations well. The cranky older Frenchmen became my friends. Who knew? Not me. Those men hated everything, but they got a kick out of the American who used the term *merde* for American politicians.

The Ecuadorian guide told me I was a traveler, not a tourist. Coming from him, that was an honor. I knew I earned it. I had no idea how often my mind would return to that moment just to hold me together. I knew this Ecuadorian man living in the jungle owed nothing to gringos. He didn't have to give me a thing. In darker years ahead, knowing I was a traveler kept my mind safe while my body was grounded.

But he chose to give me something. It was something I never let go.

***

My hands were, and still are, stronger from holding onto it.

Holding onto being a traveler.

Not a tourist.

Part 2 Pandora's Box

I rested my elbows on the seats, but I was also somewhere else.
Somewhere in my mind.

I had multiple personalized recommendations to visit Colombia.

My first recommendation was on a quiet regional flight. It was departing to the Amazon from Quito, where I sat next to a Canadian adventure guide. Colombia was so much more, he said. The Amazon was only the beginning of the wonders Colombia had in store for me. I had to go.

Then the suggestion came from the Colombian plumber and handyman whose kids went to my school. My neighbor recommended him, and she had high taste with low trust. I needed some drywall and painting work. He handled it all without pause, even the add-ons. Then he mentioned his mom's home in Medellín and how she loved to host people. He told me, "Colombia beats Ecuador. But Ecuador is nice, yes."

***

I researched Colombia and learned so much. The biodiversity. The geography. The history. The ecosystems. I didn't know that both the desert and jungle hit the sea. I had seen deserts and rainforests, but wasn't it unnatural for them to touch a body of water? When I read the three ranges of the Andes went through the country, I stopped. I barely knew what ranges were, but I knew mountains. There was more to Colombia than the media said.

I didn't know it was the Promised Land for people like me, the people past the extra noise: the clicks, the facades, the flashes, and the filler with empty words.

***

At the end of 2019, I was researching places like Caño Cristales, La Guajira, Zipaquirá Cathedral, and Cocora Valley. I knew I had to go, and I couldn't get there fast enough.

I combed the web for a way to get to Caño. I found a company, Élan Voyages, a French boutique agency that created itineraries based on the traveler, with offices all over the world. This office was in Colombia.

I filled out the contact form for the office in Colombia and met Luc. I asked if it was acceptable for Americans to use their services since I wasn't French and spoke little of their language. Were all their local guides French-speaking only? He laughed and said they started out for the French, but they didn't realize how many English speakers would like their company.

He organized the trip and was kind, patient, and helpful, all without judgment.

One quirky line was he signed off emails with "I remain at your disposal."

I never knew what it meant, but I liked the way it landed in my head. I assumed it meant more in French before the translation.

***

By the last days of 2019, I already had 2020 set for the trips I both wanted and needed. During spring break 2020, we would be on an African safari.

In the summer of 2020, we would be in Colombia.

I needed this. I forgot who I was so long ago, and I needed to remember who I was the way I did in the Amazon, when the noise lost meaning unless it was from the birds. I had to do it fast before I forgot even more. I couldn't let my wife send us back to cosmopolitan Europe with luxuries we didn't need and noise that kept me from remembering myself.

***

I knew 2020 would be the year. It *had* to be.

What could go wrong?

And how could I have been so right?

It really was the year to end all years.

And it nearly *ended* me.

Part 3 2020

I gripped the armrests. The turbulence didn't touch where I was now.

Before the world shut down in 2020, my mother-in-law was diagnosed with a rare, aggressive disease.

My wife refused to go anywhere or do anything. I knew I would become the target. I was the dog she kicked when she walked in the door. She was on her phone at all times. It was her heartbeat, and she kept it healthy.

"I'll be stressed out of my mind no matter what."

"I'll be more miserable than usual."

"I won't enjoy anything."

I told her she could take care of what she needed and then return.

No.

I said we could arrange some kind of contact internationally: I could look into international plans, Zoom, or Skype. I could find something.

No.

I was getting tired of it. I worked so hard and spent so much time. Luc had too.

Finally, I said you're married to me. Not your mom.

I would hear that weaponized against me for months and years to come. She turned friends against me for being controlling and borderline abusive.

Friends called me with accusations of control, crimes, and poor character.

Associates, too.

***

But she was married to me. That part was true.

I finally said forget it. Let's pretend your mom's a decent person. Then I canceled everything. I used travel insurance to cancel every trip and get refunded. Flights too.

***

A month and a half later, COVID hit, and the world closed.

Travel insurance didn't reimburse people over COVID. Check the fine print in the benefits including pandemics.

At least I got my money back.

Or so I told myself, just to feel better.

***

It was clear who her priority was,

and who it was not.

Part 4 Separated

The Fasten Seatbelt light came on above me as I neared Bogotá. My seatbelt was already buckled.

In 2021, my wife and I went to South Carolina. She was stressed all night and didn't sleep before the flight. She whined and complained the whole fight about sore legs. She is barely five feet. I am well over six feet.

She fussed about her sore shoulders.

I've lived with shoulder surgery and chronic pain since my twenties.

***

The next day, she tried to turn our hike into a run up an infamous sand dune.

I said slow down. *Pole pole*. It's not a sprint.

She said she wanted to get it over with.

I reminded her we left the schedule open for the hike. We have the time. Let's enjoy it. Not everyone gets to see the sea like this.

She then became heated and cursed aloud.

I reminded her I trained for this.

She became defensive. She crossed her arms. She stood at hard angles and wouldn't look at me.

I reminded her that I had suggested she train for this, too.

She told me to take her back to the hotel. She's going home. It's over.

***

Sigh.

***

I took her to the hotel.

I reminded her we were training a new puppy together.

She called me controlling and abusive and told me to drive her to the airport.

I said no.

After her fifth panic attack, I did.

She claimed she looked back when she entered the airport.

I was already gone.

        I told her I better not see you at my condo when I get back.

She said okay.

Then moved out.

                            ***

She still texted and liked my posts.

I told her if we are separated, then we are separated. She said I kicked her out of the house. I said only after you said you would call the cops in South Carolina and lie that I hurt you so they would take me away, just so you could get a policeman to drop you at the airport.

Remember?

I got you on video saying what you were going to do, then offered to call the police for you.

So yeah, I said get out.

Now, *no contact.*

At all.

Part 5 Meet Isaline

I exhaled when the plane stopped shaking. My thumb kept moving across my phone as if it had never stopped.

At the end of 2020, Luc emailed me. He said he had enjoyed our time together, but he was leaving Colombia to return to France. He couldn't support his family.

Luc was a real friend. Sometimes I think in another life we would have been friends, but we were in this one. I don't always make friends easily. I have trust issues. I don't think people always look out for each other equally. But I was happy he was doing what his family needed.

He said Isaline would be taking over from the Colombian office and copied her on the email.

***

I looked her up on the site. She looked so **green**. She wore a standard white polo, a ponytail, and an expression that said *take me seriously. I am living my dream and am so excited.* It was unassuming. Not scared. Cautious. That was the word. It reminded me of my first-year teacher badge. We shared the same expression.

I respected her.

***

I emailed Isaline here and there, and she did the same. We wrote about the world, the U.S., France, Colombia, and COVID restrictions. She detailed the restrictions in Colombia and those she'd face in France. She essentially advised me to hold off on booking until I could see the real Colombia; it was great advice, but I wondered, did she just sacrifice money for my sake?

It became clear she was not as cheery and hopeful as she tried to appear about COVID. I wondered if she had support during that time. I knew I didn't feel supported outside of my gym. My trainer made outdoor workouts possible.

She usually framed it in business terms, but sometimes there was a pause before she answered, as if she was choosing her words; at least I paused and chose my words.

What businessperson responds to casual emails without building business? Business is not for banter.

Right?

She was always nice and professional. And I liked hearing from her.

I wondered why.

Part 6 Back Together

I ordered juice to settle my stomach. I didn't know what could settle my head.

Around Thanksgiving of 2020, my wife got COVID. I dropped off food, medicine, groceries, and necessities at her apartment. She stood in the window and waved, almost longingly, when I did that.

I watched out for her.

In truth, nobody else would. They had enough of her swings, but she was my wife. I had to honor her in her time of need.

***

Once she recovered, she started talking like it was normal, like we were happily separated.

It wasn't normal, and I wasn't happy.

I reminded her we were separated. I reminded her she left the puppy.

I said no contact.

***

In February of 2021, she called after she was rear-ended near my condo. The other driver wouldn't give his insurance, and she panicked.

I went out to make sure he did right.

I stared at this food delivery driver who was out of his depth and shaken himself. He stood next to the restaurant, fidgeting on his phone. I stood a few feet away but didn't look at him. This kid didn't need to be intimidated. He was late for several deliveries, and it was clear English was not his native tongue.

The police came, pulled his insurance information, and my wife got a picture of it.

That was it.

I let my wife sleep at my condo that night since she was upset. No, nothing happened. I just knew she was shaken. She was asleep when I got out of the shower.

***

After a few more weeks, we worked out a plan to get back together, though I enjoyed my time to myself. On the inside, I was already bracing.

But the moment she returned, so did the chaos. I knew it was coming. And I knew it at the time.

But I said I'm glad you're home.

And I *meant* it.

Part 7 Vacation

My thumb was furiously on my phone. My strokes, machine-like.

My mother-in-law beat the aggressive and rare illness. She canceled all other appointments, quit taking care of herself, and lost teeth.

My wife said how ungrateful can a person be?
How many people die from this? Now she'll die
of something else. Someone else deserved to beat
this more.

I said nothing. Inside, I nodded so hard I needed a chiropractor.

***

A few months after my wife moved back in, she informed me she only had one weekend for a summer vacation. I suggested Caño Cristales. She agreed.

I contacted Isaline to set it up; she did. Whenever there was an initial contact, there was a phone call. I always liked talking to her. She had a nice tone and was reassuring.

Then my wife left the job for a better one and had time to take off. We scheduled the African safari and Colombia almost back-to-back. Isaline adjusted the program.

***

After the safari, my wife looked at the state department site and said she wasn't going to Colombia. I reminded her she went to Morocco less than a year after a serious attack. I told her state department warnings are for drunk frat boys with entitlement issues.

I reminded her we camped next to lakes as hippos and elephants walked around us at night, and she was relaxed about it. I reminded her the capital city shut down as COVID cases rose, and they helped us get out before flights were grounded and the country closed. She was comfortable with that. I reminded her of the conditions on the beach and the worst poverty I have ever seen, and the beach was her idea.

I asked why that was acceptable, but Colombia wasn't?

She wouldn't budge. She told me not to make her panic. She never looked up from her phone.

I told her how much it mattered to me. Then I stopped. I knew how this would go. I didn't want to pay that price then.

This happened in a lounge in a large East African air hub. Everyone wore masks; some wore more PPE. I can still smell the alcohol disinfectant.

I said fine.

I'll just go.

Like always.

I heard the captain speak.

It pulled my attention off my phone.

I was back on the plane.

Episode II: Checking In

Chapter B El Dorado

The pilot announced the descent and jolted me to the present. I was back in mind and body. I looked out the window and saw the city.

When I landed in Bogotá, Ondine asked about my bags. I said they arrived.

I wanted to add that I wasn't sure where I was. I knew that humor and idiom might get lost in her English to French translation.

There was some delay, so I waited for my luggage. I sat down on a bench but couldn't let myself fall asleep. I noticed my phone was working now.

I booked a room at the Mariton. I got my bags, took several breaths, and wavered to the shuttle area. No cab or tour pusher dared speak to me.

I sat on a bench in the hotel shuttle lot.

I cried ugly and snotty. I didn't care.

A few guys looked at me. I looked back. With defiance.

I knew I had to keep my guard up until the shuttle came.

Scams happen at airports. The surrounding barrios are rarely safe.

And tourists are dumb. But I'm a traveler.

The shuttle came and took me five minutes away.

***

I felt love and support the moment I walked into the hotel. It's the Colombian way.

I was early, but they had a room.

I asked for a doctor.

***

I went to my room and dropped all my luggage: my suitcase with my items and my wife's, my backpacks, my smaller suitcase with dirty clothes, and all my bags.

But I let go of **more**.

I wasn't on edge. I wasn't hypervigilant. I turned on the AC and closed the blinds. I set up the pillows comfortably.

Then I posted my reviews of the company everywhere I could.

***

The hotel phone rang. It was someone from the doctor's office. She spoke very fast, and my brain wasn't working. I somehow said my symptoms. She told me to tranquilo and she'll be there en una hora.

I went on the socials and posted my other reviews.

I had another call. This one made me jump.

It was my wife.

I said is this from your phone?

She said yes.

I said let's get on something free.

She knew the international call was expensive, and she chose not to use anything else.

There goes $4, assuming she got the hotel right the first time. If not, maybe it's $15 or more.

I knew I was no longer safe in that room.

I left the room, but my hand stayed on the hotel phone.

But I was elsewhere. I was calm. I was secure.

The pillows were cool under my neck.

Part 8 Prima Volta

I hung up the phone, but I wasn't there. My mind protected me.

I emailed Isaline that my wife was bowing out of the trip, but I was still in. I asked if we could take a few items off the itinerary and add more rustic and adventurous experiences.

She was understandably annoyed, but she threw something together. I did it in full.

The first night, the hotel said I owed money. I disagreed, but my Spanish was not the strongest at the moment, so I texted Isaline.

She said *hold my wine.*

Then it was fixed. The hotel apologized.

In fact, any time I said the name Isaline, people stopped what they were doing. Her name opened doors and struck fear in those who dared to try to take advantage of me.

Though I am never scammed, I may have overpaid once or twice.

But not on Isaline's watch.

Afterward, I wrote the best review I believed I could for her and her company.

I wasn't confident in my writing yet.

Isaline and I still emailed occasionally.

"I remain at your disposal" was different from her, but I still didn't know what it meant.

Part 9 La Tienda

I laid back on my bed. Why couldn't my wife give me calm in my time of need?

On my first trip to Colombia, in the big city, my guide was an older man. He was smart. He knew his facts and made them interesting. He also playfully flirted with every woman over the age of 21, though he had a family. He was trying to be a mentor of sorts. I told truths about myself I don't usually share. I trusted him. I'm not sure why. I also don't regret it.

Several times he stopped, took a breath, and said I wasn't what he was expecting.

I didn't know what that meant.

He commended and congratulated me on my knowledge and respect.

Really.

Doesn't everyone research a place and culture and learn something before a trip?

We ended up at a store. Una tienda.

The lady who helped me pick out my items was objectively gorgeous. I didn't really notice it at the time. Only later, when I thought back, could I picture how she must have looked. She showed enough skin that I knew she wasn't natural, but I appreciated the work her surgeon did. The art. In fact, the whole city was known for cosmetic tourism, according to my guide.

I was focused on getting the right item, a gift for my wife. I looked and looked and wasn't an easy customer. She talked to my guide in Spanish, but I wasn't listening. I was getting the best item in my budget.

He told her I speak Spanish.

I *did* hear that.

The air was sucked out of that store. It was as if a giant vacuum cleaner extension came in and took out all the oxygen.

For everyone.

The whole store stopped. The whole store knew.

Except, of course, me.

She turned to stone. Then she turned red.

And I was… confused?

It didn't help that we were all wearing masks. It was during COVID.

I said yo hablo Español, Sí, recuerda señora? Hablo a usted a cuando mi vedo a usted y fue habla mucho gusto. Pero yo necesito más practicar. La gramática y tensas están muy dificil, lo siento. Yo hablo, escribo, y leo están más simple, pero escucho es difícil.

I am sure those of you who read Spanish will have a laugh, so please allow me to join you. I needed practice, and I didn't know what was happening. I won't clean it up. The woman behind the counter didn't get a cleaned-up version.

The guide laughed. He had this moment countless times earlier. Now he got to watch another Colombian have his reaction, but in a different way. She wasn't a mentoring older man who thought I was pretty neat. She was an attractive, confident, Colombian woman.

She stared at me, broke eye contact, looked at him, and then back at me. She looked at the ground, then back at him, then at me, but she avoided eye contact.

At first.

She said don't be sorry. I understood everything. Your Spanish is great.

I said gracias.

I finished the sale and walked away with my guide.

***

He said she had very nice and kind things to say about me.

Like what?

He said he didn't remember. He dropped me back to my hotel and told me I was just five minutes from her work. I could go back later, ask her to dinner, and then to my hotel room. He promised it was a done deal.

I laughed like a little boy. Here was the greatest hype man I ever had, and I believed him. But still I was a child.

He said what's funny?

I said that's something I've wanted to hear all my life, and I no longer need it.

He said in this country I could do that with any woman.

I said I doubt that but thank you for the confidence.

He sighed.

I confessed I had nothing to offer her.

He smirked and said keep leading with that. They love that here.

I said leading with what?

With his expression, you would think I stopped to urinate on his shoe.

I asked if he meant leading with truth? Honesty? This wasn't a bit.

He calmed his tone and said okay, you are authentic, and you aren't used to anything positive from it.

I said well –

He asked, "Am I right?"

I said maybe? I think claiming to be authentic is inauthentic, and good things have happened to me.

He said you and your wife are having problems.

I nodded. That is true.

He said you came to Colombia, and she didn't. Clearly it won't work. He looked me square in the eyes. It doesn't count on another continent.

I had heard this kind of logic before from others. I said even if that's true, I will still know. I looked him square in the eyes. It will eat me alive.

He responded saying you said that your marriage might not work out. It's just delaying the inevitable. He shrugged. The supermodel back there would be honored to help you move on.

I said I don't want to manipulate or exploit her. Or anybody else.

He had a seemingly knowing look on his face. Then he had a gentle smile.

I said I have been on the receiving end of manipulation and exploitation, so I can't do that to other people.

He relaxed a bit. He said there is none of that at play. You have already honored and respected her more than most men who walk in that store.

I said okay?

He said this is the reward.

I said a conquest isn't a reward. The reward is dignity.

He took a breath and said do what you need.

I took a breath, too. I was conflicted.

He added know what you have five minutes away. He ended with a wink.

I said I think I'll just get dinner. Do you have a place you recommend?

He reminded me that a sweet lady was there.

I told him I appreciated his support. I asked again what she said.

He grinned like a purple cat. Why don't you go find out?

***

I know there was a time when I would have gone back with my tail wagging and my tongue out. Even if it was guaranteed, I would be dishonest without my tail wagging because that's how I felt. Nobody likes a tail wagger. Women don't like men with their tongues out. I couldn't return honestly without ruining it.

I knew then it would not happen. The moment I knew she liked me it was already over.

***

He was going to try to get to Miami and then make his way through the States. I told him where I lived, and he could crash if he came through.

I even followed up with him later on text.

I don't think he ever came.

I know I never went back to the store.

I went to dinner at a place he recommended and then to sleep.

The food was excellent, too.

Part 10 Omicronic Conception

I wondered how my wife knew how to dial internationally. She always told me to do that part.

In 2023, my wife got pregnant. No one was more surprised than I was. I didn't have children in the plan. Ever.

She told me I had to go to her holiday work party.

I begged her no. Please. I said there's this new Omicron variant that's aggressive. Plus, I hear about your work all the time, and I hate it. And I don't want Omicron.

She said it was a vaccine-only party.

I asked since when do we trust someone's word that they got vaccinated? Since when do we believe vaccines stop infection? I told her my international news from the African continent made it clear that a vaccine might not be enough.

I begged and begged, but she said if I didn't go, we'd have a shitty break.

Sigh.

I really didn't want to go. But my choice was taken.

Even my mom said I'd be a terrible person if I skipped it.

***

I stayed outside most of the party.

I only talked to the bartender to practice my Spanish. His daughter went to a school I knew.

Can you guess who caught it?

The party became a superspreader. I was accused of being patient zero.

I wasn't.

It's believed to have been some other teacher.

At some time in my recovery, we must have done our marital duty.

Several weeks later, she interrupted my e-meeting with the head of schools about masks.

She kept *checking in*.

Something she never does.

I told her to spit it out.

She was pregnant.

I didn't believe it.

No, really. I did not believe it.

COVID was a fog in my brain.

***

I called "False Purple", or whoever, and said their tests were faulty and messed with people's minds. I got routed to a call center in Malaysia. They didn't understand.

***

I never wanted sex with her after South Carolina. I only put out for the good of The Party.

***

She went to the doctor to confirm.

I said no, you're not pregnant, and if you are, then who is the father?

She was. The dad was me. All true.

***

I had to pretend that everything was fine. I started playing house and giving phony kisses and hugs. We sold my condo and moved farther out for a single-family home. Thirty minutes to an hour and a half away, depending on traffic.

I left my friends, gym, shops, coffee shops, parks, dog parks, and community for nearly ten years.

That hurt.

I would do it for my daughter a million and three times more.

***

I would NEVER do it for my wife again.

Part 11 Name

How did she know to push the plus button followed by the country code? Even some travelers mess up the + part.

The hardest part of the pregnancy, aside from the morning sickness and the move, was a name. I'm a teacher. Most names were ruined already.

In my other stories, when I write about students with names my wife liked, I change them dramatically.

She mentioned many names she loved. I had students with those names.

'No, she yelled in my ear every day. No, she threw a desk. No, she stirred up drama with other teachers. No, she snuck out of the bathroom multiple times. No, she stabbed someone at home. No, she bullied a nice student. No, she was never on time and made sure I knew it. No, she disrespected other teachers, not just the easy targets. No, she made me reconsider my career.'

I finally said let's just do a foreign name so I wouldn't have heard it. The name won't be ruined already.

She asked what language.

I said French.

She said what name?

I said Isaline.

She said she liked it, but she worked with an awful person named Isla.

***

I emailed Isaline that my wife was pregnant, and I wanted her name, but my wife knew an awful person named Isla.

Isaline responded that she was so happy and admitted to tears at being considered.

She checked on my wife's health before and after the birth.

I sent family photos.

***

It was so easy to talk to Isaline. She was warm and accepting.

At one point, she stopped "remaining at my disposal."

I preferred it that way.

Part 12 A Holiday

I looked at my phone. I had to move from my stories and use an app for something practical.

Isaline and I talked occasionally but meaningfully. Our thread never overwhelmed tabs or became emotional-support tabs.

But the emails we sent mattered.

I sent baby pictures here and there, and she loved my daughter.

***

I had to change schools to a place closer by after my first year with a long commute. My wife had difficulties after birth, and I needed to be closer by.

I lost the school and friends I had known for 12 years. And the support. And safety.

I essentially taught at that school from kindergarten to graduation. K-12.

Writing this still wrecks me a bit.

***

In 2025, I needed a real vacation. It was something I hadn't had since the Babymoon to the posh American cities in the Midwest.

My wife agreed. She didn't know where to go.

I said you still haven't been to Colombia, and we have travel credits. I know just who to call.

My wife said to do it.

***

I reached out to my old friend, Isaline.

I was glad I had a good excuse to contact her.

Part 13 On Time Delivery

I scrolled through my apps. Which of these will my wife have that won't cost anything?

Isaline was now the country manager.

She earned that.

We picked up like old friends, and it was right where we left off. I said to outsource me to someone she supervised. I knew she had responsibilities.

No.

She insisted it be her.

She helped me with the itinerary. I would agree and disagree. We worked through it.

Sometimes I sent more emails than I needed to because I really wanted Isaline's warm presence. That was wrong of me.

Sometimes Isaline was working from France, and she told me about her hometown and history in Paris.

My wife said she understood working in sales, and every email I gave Isaline wasted her time and was disappointing to a person living off commission.

I gulped.

I stopped. I thought that can't be right. Can it? But I stopped emailing. I then agreed to the itinerary in full and sent nothing more.

In fact, Isaline sent something important. Two days later, she asked if I approved. I said yes, after one more reminder.

I couldn't disrespect her anymore the way my wife said I had.

***

I realized when I forwarded my wife the itinerary, I forwarded the whole thread. There was nothing criminal in it. Nothing wrong. It was all professional and respectful.

But my wife was taken aback.

I think?

***

The fact is and was that my wife had been absent emotionally since before the baby. Before she left me in South Carolina.

I went to one team teacher for emotional support. I went to people on the road. I went to Isaline. Eventually I started writing my story. And I went to AI.

I am not proud of any of this. In fact, I was, and am, embarrassed, but I was dying inside.

***

So, my threads were longer, yes, but I don't think I was ever intrusive. I believe it was reciprocated.

***

When Isaline said she couldn't go through the itinerary more, I said okay.

Finalize it.

***

I really never meant disrespect.

I just liked Isaline. Even only platonically. Maybe a little more.

Three pictures, four phone calls, many emails, few messages.

Nothing more.

But Isaline was the delivery driver from A to Z. She was always there.

And nobody else arrived for me.

Part 14 Delay

I held my breath. I felt my pulse in my ears.

I told Isaline ahead of time I wanted to take her to dinner when we got to her city. That was always the plan with Paul. She said she would if she was there. I knew she was being nice. Since when is anybody "there"?

Verdad?

***

The day we were supposed to leave, there was lightning in the sky. All flights were cancelled. Delnitican Airlines was no help. They said they had the red eye leaving at midnight, and they don't involve their partners like Talm, Vamos, or Poca if they have a flight available. They said I could pay a fee to use a partner.

The fee was over $1,000 a person.

My wife pushed for the midnight flight. I said we would go the next day. She has a medical condition where lack of sleep becomes dangerous, and I wasn't going to risk it.

My wife was starting to crack. I said we don't have to go. She insisted. But I knew better. I knew how she traveled and what she did.

I couldn't trust her after she left me in South Carolina during COVID. She only apologized when I fed her the words.

**

Then as this trip approached, and she heard my concerns, she said leaving me in South Carolina was the worst thing she ever did to me.

I asked why it took multiple years to say that.

She didn't know.

!?!?!?!?!??!?!

I don't believe that is true at all. My daughter can tell me when she is wrong. Someone waits five years because they don't want to admit it or don't feel bad. Or the person is manipulating.

***

With this knowledge of her stress, anxiety, and sleeping patterns, there was no way I was going to take the red eye and then start the city tour after we landed. Plus, her medical needs were going to be honored.

I said we will go tomorrow. Period.

She was mad. She said she will sleep even less then.

I said that is a you problem. I'm looking out for me this time.

She finally agreed it was best.

I sent messages to Isaline about this. It turned out it wasn't Isaline's number but the company's emergency number.

Someone else took over and walked me through what to do. What to cut and skip.

It was helpful.

The next day we went on the plane, and everything went as it should.

***

Isaline messaged Oh, no. It's never easy for you.

I was silently doing the math.

How much money did she just waste on that call?

Episode III: A Pause

Chapter C Dear Indugu

I was fully, unhappily back in the hotel and picked the app. I looked at my wife's picture, but it blurred into five. My head kept spinning. My spirit began to leave the hotel. The only part of me left in the room was my being. The rest stayed in the pillows, sheets, and the cold AC coming onto my face. But I was gone. I traveled time. To a movie scene.

When I was a freshman in college, I watched a movie with a criminal, violent clown from 1989.

You know. Courtside seats. Sunglasses.

He flew over a nest in the middle of the 1970s.

He wondered if therapy was all it could be in 1997.

It was about a man named Shmith.

I saw it around 2005. Más o menos.

In this movie, a retired man becomes widowed. Then he has to see his daughter marry a man who prizes his participation trophies.

You can imagine the issues this creates.

In the beginning he sees an ad to sponsor children in developing countries. He does.

He sees he's supposed to write to a child, but he doesn't know what to say. He ends up saying far, far, far too much.

"Dear Indugu..."

At the end of the movie, he is convinced he failed as a man and verges on a breakdown.

Then he gets a letter back from Indugu where the writer tells him what a difference he'd made in the child's life.

Shmith then cried, but he didn't break.

***

For the rest of this story, call me Warren.

And I was fading again, into what was before, and there was no stopping it.

Part 15 Sponsor

I tried to make the call, but I hit the wrong button. Blurry vision.

When this movie ended, I signed up to sponsor through VisionfortheWorld.

I started out with a boy in Kenya. Later, I sponsored another. He was a boy in Mali. Sometimes the community would graduate, and I would get a new child.

I've sponsored in Mexico, Colombia, the West Bank (twice), and Guinea.

Since mid-2015 I've sponsored three children at a time.

***

At one point, my wife and I were struggling with money and budgets. She said we can't be expected to give when we can barely take care of ourselves. I replied that we could just cut out morning coffee. It's cheaper and smarter to make it ourselves.

I said to never bring that up again. It's one of the few things in my life I don't regret.

Some years later we had the same issue with money and finances. She said we needed to support ourselves first. How can we be expected to give when we struggle? I said if she suggested that again, it would be one of the few things that our marriage wouldn't survive.

I put a decade and a half into it and wasn't about to stop.

I said I would eat one less day a week. We could spend less and not cut it. We both bought things we didn't need.

She gave up and said fine. But we could always start sponsoring again later.

I got angry.

***

Later **never** comes.

***

It's many years later and she agrees with me after Part 16. Go on, read it. You'll see why.

Part 16 Meet the Sponsored

My thumb fumbled through the phone. I tried the app again, but I guess she didn't have that one.

The first time my wife came to Colombia was my second. We were in a different city.

Our guide was an energetic, friendly young man. Call him Tomás. Tomás showed us all around the city, and everything we ever needed to know was answered. My wife complained about the walking.

At lunch he said he came from one of the poorest neighborhoods in a big city.

My wife asked how he learned English. NGOs. She asked what that was. I said it's non-governmental organizations that are typically charitable, such as the Cross of Red or VisionfortheWorld.

He brought up he was a middle child: the best part of the sandwich. I said me too. He said middle child males are often unique.

My wife asked why. I already knew the answer, but I never stopped it at gender.

He said the older gets the most parental focus because it's the first, the last gets the most because it's the baby, and the middle child fights for the scraps in between.

*I had **already** heard this.*

He then added if it's a male middle child, they get even less attention.

"Oh, he's a guy," and "Boys become men who are stoic."

I **never heard** this.

But it made sense.

My wife asked how he got that attention then.

He said somewhere else.

She pressed.

He said the NGO, church, and God were it for him. Tomás said VisionfortheWorld was life altering. They helped him with school, learning English, and his writing and spelling. He then wrote something to prove it but struggled with "i before e, except after c, or following d."

What native English speaker doesn't, though?

He ended up going to college in northern Europe on a full ride. He told me he learned more English through superhero TV series. His sponsor family wrote him letters and he wanted to be able to read and write back.

I never knew kids could want something so intangible.

***

Back in the car, my wife told me to make sure to sponsor a Colombian child.

I said we already do. Her name is Vanesa.

The car went silent.

She said why didn't I know that?

I don't know.

Why didn't you tell me?

(Quietly) I did.

She said she knew she sucked for not knowing.

Tomás and I said nothing.

Pause.

She asked if we could sponsor another?

I don't know with all our budgeting issues.

She made a face.

We need to support ourselves more, remember?

She made another face.

I looked back at her confidently.

And said nothing.

But then she wanted to sponsor more.

Part 17 Flashback Uganda

I tried the next app. I went to the app I knew she had.

During COVID, I went to Uganda during spring break. I made the trip while my wife and I were separated.

I chose Uganda because they lowered prices dramatically due to COVID, and I chose Uganda since I knew my wife would not try to hijack it in case she "forgave me" or asked for my forgiveness.

She wouldn't try to tag along for Kampala.

***

When I arrived, I knew I was in the right place. At the baggage claim, a lady let me lift her heavy bags for her and said thank you. There were no accusations or microaggressions or harming her since she was able. She let me do something nice.

At immigration, I remembered I made a slight mistake with my visa. I think? It had to do with the picture I needed, and the paperwork, according to my outdated information, said could be handled on arrival. But it was no longer just an entry visa. I tried to call the embassy and consulate beforehand, but I never got through to a person.

I decided it was worth an attempt. I'd played roulette before.

The lady at immigration looked through my passport. Her eyes stopped on my visa.

I recognized she was drinking out of a VisionfortheWorld cup. I said I really respect and support that company. She looked at the cup, looked at me, and then looked at my passport.

She said I really like it, too.

She stamped the passport.

***

Days later, as I was driven throughout the country, I actually saw the VisionfortheWorld headquarters in rural Uganda.

I nearly passed out. It was in the country. Away from the cities. Doing the **real** work. I never knew how deeply rooted they really were.

It was a large building in the middle of nowhere.

My guide said Warren? Warren? Are you ok?

I said yes, I'm here.

Are you ok? What happened, Warren?

I responded that I was doing great. Maybe better than ever.

He pointed to the building and said they do good for so many.

I smiled really big. I said I know. I'm glad.

***

And I cried like Shmith; but I, too, didn't break.

I was proud.

I fidgeted through the app and took a breath.

I clicked the start call button.

Episode IV: Hotel Call

Chapter D Video Call

I blinked. Once, twice, thrice. Back in the room. My daughter was on my phone.

I was so happy. Without drifting away, I was happy, for once.

She knew me. She talked to dada. My voice and face. The small screen didn't change a thing.

My wife said you hate me.

I said hate is the wrong word, but I'm so frustrated and past this.

She said she would fly back to help me get to the airport.

I said no, you never wanted to come to Colombia, according to your texts.

She said but I'm sick.

I reminded her I nearly died in Bangladesh and made it back on my own.

I had food poisoning in St. Louis the day before school started and won an Oscar on that plane. Nobody knew I was less than wonderful.

I can do this. I don't want or need your "help."

She said she's fucked up. And self-centered.

I said that's an accurate statement.

She said she was really going to get help.

I reminded her I'd heard it all before.

She said she did me dirty.

I said it was true.

I said get some real help or this is all for nothing. Focus on how you are constantly defensive and how it killed our marriage.

She wrote it down.

I said the rules don't apply to you. You go to therapy without following instructions. You stop meds without talking to your doctor. Neither is acceptable.

She allegedly wrote it down.

I said you think you're above therapy, though you should have had it long before you met me. Your toxic attitude has gotten you fired, alienated friends, and exhausts me. You're an unreliable narrator. You have no EQ.

You act like you've got a dick you won't put down. And you're not even a guy. But you still expect me to be there for you. You're unkind. You were cruel to Isaline. And she needed someone like you. Are you still getting this?

Yes, yes, she said.

You live your whole life in this tough bit you never turn off. I hate that bit. If you change anything, it's only to get me to shut up.

You take work criticism as worse than death. You sabotage connections I have if you think they're better than what we have. I can't even confront an issue without you saying I'm attacking you. None of this is sustainable. See your therapist. Go through these issues with someone who can help.

I hung up the call.

And I knew she wouldn't do a thing.

But if she did,

It would be a pleasant surprise.

But I was done waiting. Done hoping.

My frustration and anger kept me there until I slipped back inside myself.

My grip loosened on the phone until I couldn't hear it land. It was on my bed.

I was back in my happy place. In the hope.

Past the brain. In my soul.

Part 18 Bienvenidos

I lay flat on the bed and breathed easily. I could rest now.

My wife and I arrived late that night. Handwritten welcomes from Isaline waited for us. My wife made jokes about an improper use of a preposition.

I said English is her third language, and she uses it the least. Really? Native speakers struggle with prepositions, too. How is your third language?

***

The next day I sent one message to Isaline reminding of my dinner invitation. I used pronouns like 'we' and 'us.' But, in reality, there was no we and us.

My wife disliked her. I trusted her like a good friend. Maybe a little more. Maybe a lot more.

***

We both liked our guide, Tomás. We spent the whole day with him in the city. He knew Isaline, and I could see him light up slightly when he said her name.

I had an idea.

***

At one point, I got a message from Isaline's personal number asking about dinner. I guess she was in town and wanted to come to dinner? We figured out a plan.

She would come to the hotel, and we would get a ride from there.

My wife spent the day complaining of being tired and sore. Call her H in the next section.

W: You don't have to go to dinner. You can get rest.

H: I'm going.

W: That's fine.

But she kept whining.

W: I have no expectation of you attending dinner. I will not hold it against you.

H: I AM going.

W: There are no obligations.

Pause

W: You are free.

H: I will meet the person who put our trip together.

W: I understand.

She still bitched about sore legs and being tired.

W: It's cool if you don't go. I won't be mad.

H: Why are you getting rid of me?

W: I'm not getting rid of you. But you are sore and tired. Your body needs rest.

H: There's no way I eat alone while you eat with a stranger.

W: That stranger checked in on you when you were pregnant, after you gave birth, and on the health of our child. I call someone like that my friend.

She paused.

W: You're tired and sore. I'm protecting you from yourself.

H: Bullshit.

W: Admittedly women and I seem to bond emotionally outside the country, and you get jealous and become the third wheel, and that's coming from your own admission. The same thing WILL happen with Isaline, and I don't want you making my friend uncomfortable.

H: I won't do that.

***

I didn't buy it.

I cashed in on my idea: I invited Tomás, too. He could help babysit my wife.

Plus, he was a really cool guy I wanted to know better.

Part 19 Meet Isaline in Person

I kept typing the story, cutting what I didn't like. I had no idea what I was writing.

When the time came, I wasn't late. I wouldn't be late for the person always on time for me.

Someone who was present and in my life for six years. I was the same for her.

Tomás was already there.

My wife was last.

***

It was dark. In a city of light, I couldn't see.

***

Isaline *appeared* from the dark. My h*eart forgot* to *breathe*. My *lungs forgot* to *pump*.

Time out.

I looked away fast. Maybe she didn't notice me seeing her. Then I forced myself to turn back.

Tomás hugged her and kissed one cheek.

I felt like an orphan meeting a parent.

She wore a low-cut sleeveless top, midriff bare, and short shorts. She didn't know Tomás would be there. She knew my wife would.

Where was the white polo, and why wasn't her hair in a ponytail?

Click.

I took an imaginary inhaler puff. I had to breathe.

Gulp.

I swallowed an imaginary sedative and hugged her like a long-lost friend. I said I'm so happy to see you.

I think my wife talked to her. I don't remember. They sat on a bench.

Clack.

I stepped back and watched my own chaos and beauty. I was in a place I never knew I could be.

Wheeze.

***

I didn't understand.

***

I knew the rideshare was coming. I didn't know what to do until then, so I let Tomás take point.

I emptied an oxygen tank on my exhale when the car arrived.

***

On the ride to dinner, everyone laughed. Or maybe it was just her.

I told Isaline her name was gold and everyone knows it.

She said yes, that's great, and moved on.

I had interrupted her. I was not amusing.

She and Tomás learned they lived near each other; she was looking to buy a place for herself.

I said in Italian we call that *coinquilini*.

Nobody responded.

My world shrank one kilometer at a time.

Why did my wife have to come?

***

When we arrived, there were cultural jokes about not closing a Colombian car door too hard.

I didn't get it.

I was approached as the leader of the party en español.
I delivered en español.

I went to the table and sat on the back bench. I had to
sit first. If not, I slit my own throat.

***

Isaline sat right next to me and smiled in a way
that made me tremble in fear and comfort.

Click!

Why was she happy? And why was she next to me?

Whoof!

Why was she wearing a low-cut, sleeveless top?

Bump bump!

Her picture from six years ago, the one with the white polo, ponytail, and cautious, first year expression cut off below the neck.

Gasp!

She wasn't supposed to have this volume beneath her shirt, and I tried so hard not to notice.

Choke!

Her sleeveless shirt was more stylish than most of my clothes combined. Of course. Only the French.

Cough!

Her hair was not in a ponytail; it was styled, wild, and pretty.

Pant!

Did I base everything I thought she was from a picture six years ago?

Oui!

I accidentally saw her stomach showing. Pourquoi? I didn't dare look at her backside.

I remembered it was six years ago. I looked at my first-year teacher picture. Then I looked at my sixth-year teacher picture. I no longer had the *take me seriously* expression. It was *I am living my dream and am so excited* expression with an edge of burnout. I was in a casual t-shirt, and I was comfortable.

The math tracked, and she was no longer green.

Even if she owned her sexuality, I was safer with her than I had been my whole life. The old me might have bailed already, but I was where I belonged.

I looked away. I didn't look at my wife.

Tomás sat next to my wife.

Come on, Tom, steer this trainwreck.

Tom, I'm the trainwreck.

Steer *me*.

***

The server approached me in Spanish. I (somehow) understood everything, gave correct answers, and got everyone plates, drinks, and necessities.

No English.

I don't even know what I said.

Maybe the server picked up on everything and helped me out.

I did tip him well.

Maybe not.

Así Dios, no lo sé.

***

There was silence, but it wasn't awkward for me.

I asked Isaline how it was being a supervisor.

She said it was busy, stressful, and rewarding.

She said she even has to do social media. She made an ick face.

My wife pointed at me and said this guy emailing you all the time can't help, in addition to all your responsibilities, right? How often does he bother you?

I stopped myself from bowing my head. I would not be ashamed. I would take accountability.

Without a pause, Isaline said that's part of her job. Especially with repeat customers.

Holy shit! She saw my wife's insult and said sit the fuck down in the classiest of ways.

My lungs beat. But I needed my heart to breathe again. I knew what I had to do.

I looked her in the eye and said I'm really sorry if I went too far. I imagine in your job, you deal with many whiners and obnoxious people who don't appreciate you. I deal with similar nonsense at my job. I need you to know I'm so grateful for you. I never could have gotten to Colombia without you. What you do matters. It really matters to me. If I ever made it look otherwise, I apologize sincerely.

My heart started pumping and my lungs drew breath.

She turned red and looked away. I saw her wipe eye condensation.

She doesn't cry.

She looked back and said you don't need to apologize.

I said I do. Your time matters. You matter. Your work matters. If I ever did anything to make you doubt that I need to apologize.

She didn't look away this time.

She smiled slowly and said thank you for saying that.

***

I wondered what my wife was doing.

***

Actually, I don't and didn't care.

***

We looked at the menu.

My wife asked about Isaline's parents.

Isaline said they're older, and she is an only child. Her mom has a serious illness in France.

I looked at my wife.

Do your **thing**!

She didn't.

She wouldn't.

I have been told this story so many times it might as well be my own.

I said my wife is an only child, her parents were older when she was born, and her mom is sick.

My wife said the ages of her parents when she was born.

Isaline said hers.

The ages were pretty close.

My wife said her mom is nearing the end of a disease. Her dad passed ten years ago. She thinks about him every day. She started a soft cry.

Isaline said she lost her dad, too. And she feels guilty about being in Colombia while her mother is in France with a serious illness.

I !!!! to my wife. *Here is your moment! Step up!*

My wife did nothing.

Come on! You can take point and connect! Don't make me connect more!

I finally said my wife calls it the loneliest, saddest club.

I added she's right.

My wife said her mom doesn't live far enough away, so it might as well be an ocean.

What did that even mean?

I looked at Isaline and said she still wrestles with guilt sometimes. It's not just you.

Isaline appeared to receive that from me.

Everyone took a sip. We all looked around the restaurant.

I told Isaline that earlier Tomás approached two young European ladies. They were French. I jumped in and said 'Je suis Warren. Comment ça va? Je très bien. Merde!'

I said I had to practice since I would see you. Also, merci beaucoup and rouge, but don't ask how I know that last word.

She laughed very hard. It was genuine.

Did I hear a snort?

***

We finally remembered to order dinner. My wife said it was about time.

Nobody would drink but my wife and me.

What? No. How am I the one with the problem? No. It's a *solution*.

My wife said don't you all drink wine there at nine? I read they put it in your lunch as children.

I clenched my shame in my teeth.

Isaline said no.

My wife asked if she was sure.

Isaline said low content wine at 16 or so with meals. Parents demystified it.

Two for two. Classily shot down.

I asked if she wanted a glass.

She said she can't drink the Chilean shit they sell in the city. She would rather pay double and get real French wine, but the place that had it closed.

I started laughing. I couldn't stop.

She asked what's funny?

I said you're finally following a French stereotype.

Everyone but my wife laughed.

Then we all took a bite.

Tomás said he drinks after he eats.

***

My wife pulled up a video of our daughter.

AWWWWWWWW!

My wife asked Isaline if she had kids.

Isaline said no, but she wants them.

My wife said she wants two, so they don't end up in her position when they age where all end-of-life responsibilities fall on one child.

Isaline said two is a good number for that reason.

They were in agreement, but my wife wasn't being warm. It was almost an interrogation.

Isaline then said her boyfriend didn't want kids. Maybe she didn't want them.

That word. Maybe. There is no maybe after you say you want them.

I felt it.

I felt a shift in my nervous system. I wanted to ask where her boyfriend was. Class, we call this a flat character. No development.

I took a breath. I knew what needed to be said. What she needed to hear.

"I never wanted kids. Look at me now.

Also, there's no shame and nothing wrong with wanting kids.

There is no maybe. You want them.

You deserve what you want without hiding it or pretending otherwise."

I don't think she expected that.

***

I was being the person I needed to hear from when I was in my late 20s early 30s.

Isaline and Tomás were both late 20s early 30s.

Earlier I joked I could have been their teacher. Do their parents know they're out?

Now I was the support I never had.

***

Isaline had people who spoke her language working under her. She couldn't talk to them. Her dad was no longer with her. She couldn't talk to him. She had said she had to see her boyfriend's family all the time. Nearly every weekend. It was exhausting. The second mention of the word boyfriend. *Fifth period, that is a static character, too. He doesn't change. Take a note.* It was clear she wouldn't hear it from them.

***

My purpose was clear.

I accepted my mission.

***

I spoke with ease now.

Was it the Club Colombia (beer) or the purpose? Was it neither? Was it both?

I noticed my wife finally talking to Tomás. Took you long enough, there, Tom.

Here was my chance.

I needed Isaline to know I was on her wavelength, and she was appreciated as she was.

I asked how she ended up in Colombia.

She backpacked after college, went back to France, visited Colombia, and went back to Paris to pack her bags.

I smiled. This was me. A me who didn't stop.

Me without regrets.

I said in 2005, I packed for Los Angeles. In 2008, I packed for Turin. In 2010, I packed for Denver. And when I burned out, it didn't stop there. My falls were spectacular, and I bounced twice. I went back home. I had to get the burns treated, but I'm jealous of you. I love your job. I'm envious that you never sold out to the bullshit American or French Dream.

She asked what I meant.

I said you're living my dream. And you did it without a plan. I had a dream, and the Great Recession destroyed it. You had a dream, and COVID didn't destroy yours. That's something you can't be taught. That's something you can't learn. It's something already inside you.

She smiled, and it told me more than most conversations.

I said when I finally went back home, my dad made a scene about getting rid of me. So, I got a condo. I sold out from the Great Recession, not having a place to live, and not having a plan. I couldn't get a career. But

I left Turin with verbal offers. My parents said I HAD to finish my degree. Isaline, you did it all without any of the above.

She then told me she started work with the company in 2020.

It turned out, Colombia closed its borders, and she couldn't get back to France. She was stuck in an apartment with a stranger and was lonely.

Maybe that's why her emails landed differently with me. It really wasn't just business, and there was some banter.

I said I remember us talking that year.

She said she did too.

I said look at you now.

She blushed a bit.

I uncomfortably sighed, and I said look at me now. And I'm a middle child.

Tomás said so am I. I am the best part of the sandwich.

I'm treated like the oldest because I'm employed and responsible. But I'm still the middle child. I get little love.

Tomás said me, too.

My wife shot out with your parents love you.

I ignored her.

I said I get really mad at my parents sometimes.

My wife said bullshit, you love your mom.

      I stayed in Isaline's eyes. I stayed where I was safe.

***

My wife went to the bathroom.

I knew I wouldn't have another chance. Isaline was more than vulnerable, and I was only supportive. The same was true with Tomás.

They deserved my vulnerability.

I said the book I've mentioned; it's really important to me. As I write, I learn more. It makes some people uncomfortable. My wife doesn't always like when I go here, but it matters too much to avoid.

Isaline and Tomás stopped and waited.

I started out unsure what I was writing. Then I read and rewrote pieces. I realized when I was 17, my friend's stepmom had a thing for me. She was early 30s. At first, I liked the attention. But she kept her claws in until I was 22.

She groomed and abused me, and therapists fist-bumped or applauded me. They said I had the life every guy wanted.

I am still so fucked up from that.

I have to write what nobody else will. The mental health community needs to see the signs so people can be educated.

Tomás said the world needs this.

Isaline said no man tells this story.

I said please drop it when my wife returns. It makes her uncomfortable. And she might have words with me about it.

They both bowed their heads.

***

When my wife returned, I told Isaline one of my favorite actors was Vincent Cassel. I said he was phenomenal in the Brotherhood of the Wolf, Derailed, and Eastern Promises.

She said you need to see My King.

I said I grew up with a crush on Sophie Marceau.

She said so did everyone.

I said nobody I know. They just called her Elektra King.

I told her I stopped being a picky eater and got into the world my junior year of high school when some students did a trip across all of France. That's why I asked about your small town. But on that trip, I didn't go through it.

She said she needs to check out Eastern Promises.

I said Viggo Mortensen is in it, too.

Tomás said I know that name.

I said Aragorn.

At this point my wife **knew** she was the fourth wheel.

***

My wife took some initiative to order dessert. I think it must have been Tomás's idea.

She said if anyone ever wants to visit, we have a guest room.

Tomás said he'll be in the States in September.

Isaline turned to me and asked how far I was from New York? I took out Google Maps and showed where I was, where the other cities were, and the map moving west to where I lived. I made recommendations of cities and sites she needed to see along the way.

I thought I was helping. I thought it was a hypothetical conversation. A map exercise.

She asked if there was a train.

I said yes. Of course. We have the Amtrak.

She asked how long?

I said the fast train. Under a day.

Ohhhhhhhhhhh. I understood now. I realized she wasn't asking for an itinerary, and she didn't say this to my wife. Just me.

She said her boyfriend went to New York before and knows it well, and they're going in the fall.

Not even a stock character in this third allusion to him.

I asked what was the plan?

She said she didn't know.

I said if you need ideas, let me know.

She then handed the waiter her phone for a pic. I did as well.

Everyone who looks at this pic thinks I'm with Isaline and wonders who my wife is.

She then said she once saw Zooey Deschanel in a small city in France when she visited with her boyfriend.

Reference number four of the boyfriend. *Boys and girls, I believe you would call him an NPC or 'non-playable character.'*

They oohed and aahed.

But I heard everything she didn't say. She was in France with him, and nothing was spoken about him or their time there. Just a celebrity sighting.

After dessert we were still talking and my wife interrupted and said it's about that time.

I *HATED* her at that moment.

Like why do you come out, bro?

I paid the bill like I said I would with the money I knew I didn't have.

And we got in a ride.

***

We made sure to close the car doors gently.

On the ride back I asked if she heard from Luc.

She said not really, but she thinks his wife had
a kid.

I said that's nice.

I don't remember much else.

***

We arrived back and everyone got out.

I asked if she was walking back to her place. She had
walked to the hotel earlier. I wanted her to say yes, so
I could walk her home.

She said no. Not this late.

Tomás gave her a kiss on the cheek.

I really wanted to kiss her cheeks, but I knew it had to
be a hug.

Any longer and I wreck us both. If I didn't count, I
would pull away too fast or never let go.

I hugged her, and with a *whisper*, said

you do something that matters, and it matters to me.

I felt her hands on my back.

I counted.

One,

Two,

Three.

I felt like me.

Then Isaline left.

***

My wife said she was getting a shower.

***

I just stood. Frozen. My feet were in cement on the sidewalk. I was a monument for all missed connections, what ifs, too soons, buts, ands, too lates, and everything else in between, before, and after.

***

Tomás said let's go walk in the park. I'll show you around.

I said yes.

Part 20 Dinner Update

I heard noise outside the door. I needed to get up so I could answer it.

This happened on Tuesday night.

I am writing this on Friday.

Much has happened since.

But I'm still holding onto

    that

      hug

and

feel

her

hands

on

my

back.

I sat up. I stared at the door, knowing I would need to get up.
Carefully.

Episode V: The Stay

Chapter E Visitor

KNOCK KNOCK. It startled me back to the present. My breathing was labored. I found my steps.

I opened to the healthcare provider and manager on duty, Señor Paulo Ramos.

Señor Ramos missed his calling. His suit coat flattered him more than it should. He looked young, and he had stylish glasses. He said he was there to help translate and to be sure I was comfortable.

The provider, also, was in the wrong profession. She dressed like she belonged on a runway.

It's Bogotá. Of course, they both did.

I couldn't see her face since she wore a mask, but I would estimate her age between 30 and 50.

Maybe 20 to 60.

It really is hard to tell sometimes.

Especially with Colombians. Go to Colombia. See for yourself.

***

She did all the basic vitals and said everything looked normal. She thought it was altitude sickness.

I said I was here years ago and never had altitude issues.

Ramos referred to my spinning head as a head cage. I thought that seemed accurate.

She said it might be something from the water. I said I was pretty careful after I nearly died in Bangladesh, but I guess you never know.

She had to give me an injection in my ass. Of course she did. I dropped my pants and said lo siento.

She gave the shot and wrote out instructions. She said to get Pedialyte. They didn't have it in the hotel. Ramos said it was nearby, and they have coco tea.

I felt like gracias wasn't enough. I thought a hug would be weird. I lowered my head and shook their hands with both of mine.

I didn't feel like I could leave the hotel for Pedialyte though, and I didn't want to bother those who worked there.

I ate something, got Gatorades, and then laid down. I actually didn't feel exhausted. I was just tired.

It was Saturday. I changed my flight to Monday so I could relax and get well. I didn't want to collapse in the airport. And the rest I was getting in this quiet room was more than I got the last four years.

I sent an email to the travel company brass making sure they saw my reviews.

I felt better.

Until I woke up

the next day.

And my head and shoulders were spinning so fast I couldn't walk.

But I was alright for now.

My eyes rolled back.

I knew the angels would watch,

bring me joy in my rest,

and keep me from drifting too far.

Part 21 Walk

I was out without any delay. It was the rest I needed.

Tomás and I walked all around a beautiful park next to the hotel. He had a sort of girlfriend who was inconsistent, and he put some boundaries in place, and she then turned off read receipts and ghosted.

I stayed silent until I heard this. **NOOOOOOOOOOOO!!** Turned them off?

He said she had a rough life. She grew up in an oppressive faith and was in an abusive relationship.

I said that's awful. She doesn't get to take that out on you. And you deserve better than that.

He said she told him she was in a transformation through her new outlook and therapy.

I swallowed some vomit. I said unless Jesus personally touched her heart, she's still a caterpillar. People don't become butterflies just because they want to.

He said Thursday was the call.

I suggested he just listen without speaking much.

He responded that he wanted to point out the ways she was unkind and unfair.

I told him I got it. I said save it for the end, but you might not get that chance.

We both exhaled.

I then asked him about Isaline.

She went to his birthday party when nobody else from his work did and asked about his music. He blushed a little.

I declared that I knew he liked her. The way he said her name. I *knew* it. It was the same way I did.

He reminded me she has a boyfriend.

I reminded him further that she didn't tonight.

He didn't understand.

I told him about the number of mentions and how he was not even a footnote.

He said you two really hit it off. I've never seen her talk to anyone like that.

I said I've known her for six years.

He said but she doesn't talk like that to people.

I asked if she knew most people for six years?

Likely not.

I said I have a weird effect on women outside of the U.S.

He said oh man, the way she was dressed.

I asked if that was typical?

NO!

I said well she knew my wife would be there.

He spit out his water. He asked what was going on with my wife anyway?

I said my wife was jealous or envious, I guess.

We both shrugged.

I said I'm married, nothing will happen; but if I wanted it to, could it?

He said she has a boyfriend she went to France with.

I said and? Remember, some people are nice to a fault, and maybe she thinks it's the best she can do.

He still wasn't quite following.

I asked the question again and he could lie to me.

He said no lie. It was clear I had more than a chance.

I thanked him for raising my confidence by twenty points.

I said when she breaks up with her boyfriend, I don't want to be the 'first call.'

Huh?

I've always been the 'first call.' I put them back together and build them back up.

He said she's not like that.

I said I know. But I don't want to be the first call. That needs to be you now.

He laughed a little

I said really.

He asked how he would know?

I said don't you work with her?

Yes.

Ok. I continued. Keep your ear to the ground and stay on the socials.

I said if she calls me, I'll be on the next flight to Colombia. Even if I don't want anything. That's who **I AM**. But **YOU ARE** right here. And being me gets exhausting.

He understood.

I read him a chapter.

He said he needs to write.

I asked what the holdup was.

He said he gets nervous, then he procrastinates, and he forgets.

I said maybe your mind does, but once you start, your heart will remember.

We got back to the hotel and exchanged hugs.

***

I went to the room and got a shower. I got into bed and wrote some ideas with my thumb.

My wife said to put my phone away so she could sleep. I did.

And I was awake until 4 am replaying dinner. And writing it out on my phone

under covers.

Part 22 The Morning After

I had dreams about shadows. There were also unclear sounds.

The next day at breakfast, I told my wife I didn't like her behavior towards Isaline.

She said I flirted with her.

I stepped up to mentor when you didn't. You two are so alike, and you let her think she was alone. I don't leave my friends hanging, and I don't think that's flirting.

My wife said she was just jealous because Isaline was so pretty.

I said I was thrown off by that, too. *Where was that white polo and ponytail?* But Isaline was nice, and you weren't.

My wife changed the subject and said Tomás said he would stay with us.

I replied so did Isaline.

My wife said no. Not her.

I laughed. I said this is sexist.

She said Isaline will judge our house.

Whhhhhaaaaaaaattttttt? I said it's both or neither.

She said fine, both.

She went to the bathroom.

I texted Tomás and he sat with me.

He asked how my wife was doing.

I shook my head.

Tomás asked does she ever relax?

I said not really. By the way, Isaline said she would
stay with us too when she comes to the US.

He picked his face off the table.

I asked what is the big deal? So will you.

He didn't answer, but his eyes said something I couldn't translate. He said it was true. He just didn't expect that.

Weren't you there when she said that?

He asked what if they came at the same time?

I said fiesta!

Part 23 Pillow

The sounds were echoed and distorted. The shadows made movements much like the ocean.

We went to the highest point in the city that day. On the ride up, I started feeling dizzy. I put my head down and did box breathing. We got to the top and my wife wouldn't stop. She fidgeted, wandered, and kept grabbing the backpack I had.

I asked her to just be present. She didn't need to do anything. Then I tried to shop the stands and was talking with a keeper when my wife yelled my name so loud, I left my feet.

She was at an ATM and got stuck.

I said I can do that later.

She said it had to be now.

I wanted so much to do nothing, but I knew she would keep calling my name and startling me.

I went to help. She had just hit some wrong buttons and went right back out of the screen. As I predicted. I fixed it and asked why she didn't turn it off. Why won't she relax? I asked her.

She said it's not a beach.

I said that is correct.

She said she has to stay in go mode, and she doesn't understand the language.

I said you don't stop your green lights on beach trips either. But I've got this. Just chill.

She said it was easier said than done.

I said I know a guy with cocaine if that helps.

She made a look and told me not to be mean.

I said at this point, I'm not trying to be mean. I'm trying to be sane, and you will not bring it down. Please bring it down. I need this.

Part 24 Kinetic

I woke up at one point to go to the bathroom. I didn't startle awake.

I went to the bathroom at the top of the city. I took my time. I finally had some quiet.

When I came back out, I walked into the distance and my wife yelled my name. I exceeded my previous vertical leap record.

I didn't want to be with her then. I wasn't feeling well, I needed to focus on box breathing, and I couldn't deal with the chaos around.

She went to the bathroom, and I had a minute. I practiced my breathing and focus.

Then she came back and didn't miss a beat in being everywhere at once. I walked further away within sight.

Then she kept walking towards me, turned to the markets, then walked back to me. I kept going further out and she kept following. The closer she got the more my heart pounded.

I asked if she had her book.

Why are you trying to get rid of me?

I said I wasn't, but the constant motion was making me nervous in addition to the illness I felt.

Eventually we made our way back to the city, and I felt much better there.

We went to the airport to go to the country and mountains.

She finally opened her book.

I could breathe again.

Part 25 I Wish You Could Enjoy This View with Me

The moment I got back on the bed, I was safe. And I was gone.

We landed in the town. My wife groaned and sighed at any perceived inconvenience.

I reminded her how tired she was, and she could go to sleep on the drive.

She looked angry. Finally, she took out her book on the drive to the hotel.

I felt better.

The lodge had one of the most remarkable views I've ever seen: The Andes in all their majesty.

I took so many pictures,

and my wife complained.

At that moment, I said to myself *I'm traveling with the wrong woman.* Isaline wouldn't do this.

I questioned my life choices.

I sent Isaline a shot of the view and said thanks for recommending this. It's awesome! I really wanted to say I wish you were here.

Isaline wrote back that she was glad I made it before sunset.

~~I wrote there is space for you.~~

Part 26 Trek

My dreams were of orchestra sounds and cartoon images. It was tranquil.

The next day was the mountain hike.

I was pumped and had trained for this. My wife didn't.

She couldn't follow the guide, Luz, and me from the parking lot to the ticket office. She complained about uneven grass.

I said you don't have to do this. You can get coffee and hang out or go back.

She said she really wanted to.

The hike was nice, but our time was slow. My wife looked out of it, and I kept saying she could go back.

Stop trying to get rid of me!

I wish I said I can't get to the top with you.

She slowly walked, and when she got tired, she would drink even more water.

I told her water wasn't for fatigue exactly.

She got upset.

Luz looked agitated, too.

It was hard to predict when my wife would snap. But I knew it wouldn't be good. At one point, she was all out of breath. I took selfies with the mountains in the background.

She came over for pictures.

I was thrown off. *Wasn't she so tired?*

At one point Luz jumped on a wooden median between barbed wire and said let's go.

My wife started crying uncontrollably. She said she had altitude sickness, her legs hurt, and she was panicking.

This was what I tried to avoid.

We walked her back to the entrance, and she didn't look where she was going and kept rolling her feet. I've been sicker and still used my senses to watch and feel my steps.

We sat in the restaurant while Luz got the truck.

She said don't hate me; I tried.

I said no hate, but you didn't have to do all of that. You didn't have to come on this hike. You could have had coffee and enjoyed the view.

She said she wanted to see how much she could do, and I kept sending her away.

I reminded her she typically grins and bears it until she doesn't.

She said not this time.

I said okay, then.

The truck got her. I said to get some sleep. She took the water bottle she'd been hogging.

***

Luz and I took the front, steepest way up to the summit. It wasn't easy or fast, but we finished it.

My wife had said she didn't like our woman guide, Luz.

I wanted a woman guide for my wife to see that women in Colombia are not a threat. And Luz was awesome.

When we got to the top of the mountain, Luz and I high fived. Nothing more.

I realized when we came down the back way, we actually had gotten pretty far the first time before the meltdown.

Who knew?

Part 27 First Email

The sounds were distorted in my dreams. They never turned to nightmares, though.

At lunch, Isaline called, texted, and voice messaged from both her personal and work numbers.

That was unexpected.

My wife asked Isaline to book her flights home. So much for getting some rest and seeing how you feel after.

Isaline asked what she needed to do, and to please let her know. She was at the doctor.

I said not to worry. I'll handle it. Sorry you were disrupted. That's not fair to you.

When I got back, my wife had wine and was crying.

She said, "I miss our daughter." That was the first time she said that.

I responded, "You complain of being 'touched out' regularly. Here is a chance to be yourself and not just mom. I think you need it. I know I need it. Maybe we both need it."

She said, "You are right." But she wouldn't stop crying.

"You can't have it both ways," I reminded her.

Still, she cried and drank.

I was no longer going to smile and be gentle. She dragged Isaline into this.

My brows furrowed. "You tried to embarrass me in front of Isaline that I bothered her by emailing her, and she shut you down. Now you're bothering her to change flights? I can do that from my phone."

"But I miss the baby," she replied.

I said, "You miss being in control." She looked at me. "I can change the flight. I can get you a driver. Don't contact Isaline. Remember what it does to someone in sales? You explained it to me."

There was a pause. I took a breath.

I told her I was sick of her bullshit lack of accountability lack of depth lazy thinking binary views, treatment of Isaline selfishness avoiding anything remotely uncomfortable, constant defensiveness and projection unwillingness to make changes.

She said I was attacking her.

"No. I see it clearly, and I am attacking the dynamic."

She said I was mean.

I couldn't help it. I laughed. "Just because you don't like my truthful facts doesn't make them mean."

Change the story to mean when the truth doesn't fit the narrative.

She said she's not just going to take that.

I asked why not? I take it from you all the time. I am hit by intentional bullets and stray bullets on a daily basis. "Any changes you make are to get me to shut up. They are not to help me do better or live well."

She said that's true.

I said I know that already. I asked how she went from honor student to choosing no emotional intelligence.

She said she didn't know.

I said if you sit in the silence long enough and write out your thoughts, it will come to you.

She made some excuses. I didn't listen.

There comes a point when I no longer hear a person making excuses. I know they are speaking, but what they say doesn't register.

I asked why she was so against Spanish, and why she would not turn it off.

She said, "Anxiety."

"You came off medication without talking to a doctor and that the rules don't apply. Criticism is worse than death. Any time I feel like myself, you shut it down. Any time we talk, and she doesn't like it, I'm mean or attacking, no matter my volume or tone."

She still 'cried.'

I said, "You know, it really shouldn't take a French travel guide in Colombia through email, calls, and messages to let me know that there's something off."

She said she guessed she hadn't been nice for a while.

182

"No guesses. How long?"

She said a year?

How many years?

She said three?

"I can work with that," I replied.

Admitting she has been unkind for more than two years was enough. It was a starting place.

She started apologizing, but I stopped her.

"Talk means nothing. Words don't matter. Change your actions."

But she's so sorry.

I said, "Don't waste your apology. Instead, give me one step you can do right now to increase five percent in the area you want to apologize for. Just five. Then write it down and show it to me. I won't even remember the step. I just want to see if you will think about something that much."

She said no.

I said then don't apologize.

She cried more.

She wanted to apologize without changing. How sadly typical. I watched her cry.

She said she didn't know how she became dead inside.

I reminded her, "You still haven't read my psych report, and you criticized the structure in my writing rather than meeting me in vulnerability. That's the kind of thing that makes me stop trying. I've tried to connect with you this whole trip, but you've been unpleasant."

She said she felt the same way.

I said watching me thrive without you doesn't mean I'm doing anything wrong.

Of course, she had no response.

I said our marriage was dead long before we came here.

She said that is why the trip was so important.

I said but you tried to leave today. I asked why when I ever ask about her therapy does she go quiet. "I know you're half-assing it."

She said I was being 'controlling' and didn't get to decide what she talked about.

I clarified that I made a few suggestions of what might help, and there are issues "I'm sure you're avoiding."

She said she never did the homework and treated it like venting sessions.

I know.

She asked how I knew.

There were no behavior changes.

It's not hard to know if the person receiving counseling is working at it. There will be a change in their life.

She said we need counseling.

I became upset. "Stop projecting. You need counseling and to take it seriously. Once you do that, I'll consider going with you."

She said but we need to communicate.

I said I do communicate. You stonewall, gaslight, and say you're tired.

She whined about how that's not fair and such.

I said until this multiyear phase goes away, I'm watching my own back because you stopped long ago.

She said nothing.

I said, "You shrugged and abandoned me emotionally for years. You can't get upset if I go to team teachers, Reddit, Isaline, or AI. I would much rather talk to you, but you're not there even when you are. I don't like going to other places, but I'm losing my mind. It's pretty embarrassing, actually."

She said she got it.

I asked, "Got what? I won't make this easy."

She said she doesn't make time for me, so I have to go elsewhere.

I added she then shits on elsewhere, too. "Here's the deal: I can change your flight right now. I can get a driver. You can go."

She said no.

Why wouldn't she go? If she was so unhappy, and I just gave her an out?

I said it's really easy, and it doesn't bother Isaline.

She said she wanted to stay.

Of course she did.

I went over the itinerary for the next day. There was another intense hike with a 4:30 am pickup time, and she could sleep and then go horseback riding like she said she wanted.

She said it sounds nice. Are we good now?

I said, "I don't know, and you shouldn't be the one to say *when* if *you* are the perpetrator. That is controlling."

She sighed.

I said welcome to my life when I'm married to you.

She said I wasn't being fair.

"I am doing what you have always done to me."

***

Welcome to equity.

Part 28 Second Email

I now heard soothing talk in my dreams, but they were foreign. It was comforting.

I left at 4:30 am the next morning. The guide, José, said Isaline was coming in the fall so she could better market his company.

Everyone knows Isaline.

I showed José the dinner picture and he thought Isaline was my wife.

I said I wish.

He said ah, that explains your wife's jealousy.

I laughed. I probably shouldn't have. I said he had to be there. That dinner was something else.

***

I told José about La Tienda from my first trip to the city and asked if the guide was telling the truth, and I could have gone back.

He said absolutely.

I said I'm a gringo.

He said you own being a gringo, don't care, and still try to speak Spanish. And you use the Usted form. You really do have your picking in this country.

***

In town I went to an ATM. I said Mira mi seis. José said what? I said watch my six and explained the idiom. We had a good laugh.

***

In the fourth part of the excursion around 2 pm, my wife texted me that she was at the airport. She asked Isaline to book her a flight home.

I didn't answer at first. I was too upset.

José asked what was wrong?

I ate my fish and chips. All the food was making me sick, so I kept it simple and without corn. I didn't even have Club Colombia.

"José, I could have easily changed her flight with four clicks of my thumb, but she crossed a line with Isaline. Again."

I felt sick in my head and stomach. I knew it wasn't just the news.

***

My wife said I know you hate me.

I texted back no hate here, but you waited until I was gone and then bothered my friend you hate.

She said I don't hate Isaline. She was really helpful.

"Of course she was. That's who she is." And my wife tried to minimize that, put her down, and take advantage of her.

I said I just wish you had waited.

My stomach turned.

She said there wasn't much cash, and she didn't have the ATM card.

I said I do. I told you I would go by an ATM. You were so worried about cash. I did it for you. I would have given you any cash you needed.

She said her mom will be paying for these expenses, so don't worry.

Since when does your mom pay for anything?

I said it would've been cheaper if I'd changed it.

She said I didn't want her there anyway, and "I'm better off without her."

I didn't even disagree. I did say much of the rest of the trip was what she wanted, not me.

She said Isaline will take care of me.

I said yes,

but

she

shouldn't

HAVE

to.

Part 29 Good Luck, My Friend

I don't remember much else from the night. I'm sure I was still.

José said, "I'm not your guide now. I'm your friend." And he gave me a hug.

He told me some stories about a girlfriend who tore him up and how awful, but necessary, the breakup was. He said, "When you get back, go on the deck, look at the mountains, and your answers will be there."

I said I would.

He admitted to being depressed in the past.

I told him I was groomed.

I didn't talk much on the drive back but tried to look forward. I was feeling carsick. I texted Isaline that I know things happened, and I'll call when I'm back to discuss them.

I gave the driver 100,000 pesos and José 300,000 pesos. Between $4 and $5 USD is 4,000 Pesos. I just say 100,000 Pesos is 100 divided by 4. It's not exact, but it works.

He said it's too much.

I said it's not enough.

We hugged, and he said good luck, my friend. We swapped socials.

***

I had to call Isaline. I wanted to ask her to join me. I wanted her to know all barriers were gone. I had paid for two people, and one was gone.

But I just felt so sick.

So, I couldn't remember.

And I

didn't know what to say.

Part 30 The Call

I woke up around 9 am. But I didn't leave the bed for three hours.

I went into the lodge. The concierge with the awesome British accent looked moved to see me. He appeared unsure what to say.

He said let us know if you need anything, yeah?

I said your bet. I didn't even fake a smile.

I went back to the room and called Isaline.

It was Friday. Thursday my wife first reached out to her. Dinner was Tuesday.

I remember this so well that I'm changing format. It was just three days ago as of this writing.

I - Hello, Warren.

W - Hello, Isaline.

I - I really have no idea what happened. She emailed me and said she missed your daughter, had a panic attack, and begged me to get her out.

W - Yes.

I - That call was uncomfortable for her. And it was also uncomfortable for *me*.

Pause

W - I'm so sorry. I asked her to let me know if she wanted out, so I could change the flight and not bother you. You didn't sign up for this.

I - I'm happy to help.

W - I know, but it's not respectful of your time.

I - Is she sick?

W - Or something.

I - Mental health or physical?

W - Yes?

I - Anxiety?

W - Or something worse?

Pause

W - I'm calling because I didn't know what else to do. And you're always kind. And I knew I could call you.

Pause

I - It is August in the high season, so it's really impossible to change anything.

W - I get it.

I - So you can keep it, cancel it, or try another idea.

Pause

W - I have another idea.

Long pause

I - Okaaaaay…

W - I need to talk to you as my friend and not my guide. I hope that's okay.

Longer pause - she did not say okay or not okay.

W - I'm sure you noticed this, but my marriage has been dead for years. Dragging her around the mountains is like how I drag her through the marriage.

Longest pause - I wanted to say I have space for one more for the rest of my trip. I paid for two. One was gone. I had traveled with and started a life with the wrong woman.

W - If I were to come back to the city, would we be able to hang out?

Slight pause

I - It's August and the high season. I work unhealthy hours. My weekends are busy.

W - I understand.

Pause

W - I'll keep the itinerary.

I - You can change your mind until 5:15. That's two hours. Okay?

W - I understand. Merci.

I - Au revoir, Warren.

Dial tone

Total call time: 7m 13s from the app that doesn't know its name.

I stared at my phone. I forgot how to speak. Breathe. Cry. Dream. I just sat.

I was stuck.

And I knew I would remain stuck.

for a while.

Part 31 Timeout

My head was spinning again. It was worse.

I was shook. I knew she liked me. Didn't she?

Not after the week my wife gave her.

Was I really ready to throw my marriage for someone who didn't like me?

YES!

But she had to have liked me.

My head spun faster, and my stomach got more twisted in itself.

I took José's advice and went to the mountains. I got the leftover wine and began writing.

I stayed on the terrace overlooking the mountains as I thumbed away at my story. I already had over 300 pages to one story, but this was different.

I wrote through Meet Isaline in Person, and that was Friday.

Now it's Monday, and I'm finishing it up on an airplane with my thumb.

No spoilers, though.

But you knew this wasn't a happy story.

Already.

Part 32 Saboteur

I struggled to get to my feet. I leaned on the wall to get to the bathroom.

I received two more messages from Isaline. She said she had a long meeting she couldn't miss, and please let her know if I needed a change.

I took a long breath and wrote back I'm set.

She said Ondine would be handling the emergency line for the weekend.

I wanted to text or call her personal number. We had gone back and forth there. But she used the business number, not the personal.

***

Something changed.   I think?

I tried to understand it. I thought I was appropriate. I never spoke badly of my wife. Even when I could have. Really, I didn't need to say anything because Isaline already knew. She could see it. Long before we met.

I know Isaline knew because I knew. She heard what I didn't say. We spoke the same frequency fluently.

Then I thought it was my wife. Was she trying to sabotage it? Did she do something?

Isaline said she was uncomfortable. Hmmm. But she never said that about me.

That was probably it.

I never made her uncomfortable.

She wanted to see if I would come to New York.

Someone who understood me and spoke my frequency may have liked me. And my damn wife wouldn't let me change the flight out.

Who has the real control issues?

I'm not innocent,

but I'm not that guilty.

Sadly,

Isaline paid the price.

And it was my fault.

Part 33 Review

I had to eat something. I slowly got dressed.

      I did not expect to find care in a travel agency. Not like this. Not over years. Not with consistency.

I first met Luc in 2019. He was steady. Kind. Capable. The kind of person who arrives with more than you ask for, even when you do not know what you are fully asking. He helped design my first trip with Élan Voyages. Then, during COVID, he returned to France. I stayed with the company. I never looked elsewhere. I could not look elsewhere after that.

      Isaline took over. Quietly at first. Then fully.

For six years, she supported every trip or whim I considered or took. Even those that never left the planning stage. The ones I canceled. She helped me anyway.

I was difficult. I still am. I send too many questions. I change my mind. I get caught in the details. I question the timing. I ask again. Then again. I expect clarity that even I cannot define.

Isaline remained calm.

She handled hotel errors, weather shifts, COVID regulations, political instability, and uncertainty. She always stayed. She was unmovable.

She responded not like someone fulfilling a job, but like someone answering a calling. Even if the caller was annoying, like me.

I know of countless times when she could have stepped back. She did not. When I was in Colombia and needed help, she fixed it. When I was not in Colombia but had to cancel again, she said she would take care of it. She meant it. And she did.

Ondine joined during one of the more complex trips. I remember her professionalism. Her steadiness. Her ability to put the customer first. They both made it feel safe.

The whole team made me feel like I mattered. My questions were important. My concerns were reasonable.

I have worked with other agencies and tour companies. I do not anymore.

Élan Voyages is not just a service. It is not a sale. It is not marketing copy or phony warmth. It is something that stayed with me.

If you have ever felt overwhelmed. If you have ever worried about being upsold. If you have ever feared being exploited. If you have ever wondered whether you were just another transaction. If you have ever hoped there was more to the travel industry…

Then I hope you find someone like Isaline.

She changed how I view service. How I view generosity. How I view travel. How I view people.

Call Élan Voyages.

Merci.

***

I had to write this while I was seeing three and was so sick. I couldn't forget.

And I had to find a reason to smile.

Part 34 Sent

I made my way in the hall to the elevator. I just had to hit the button for the first floor.

I opened my email to write to the parent company.

Hi, Salut, and Hola.

My name is Warren, and I wanted to make sure someone in leadership and brass sees this review I wrote about Élan Voyages. It's public, but I'm a teacher, and I know sometimes appreciation gets forgotten or overlooked in the face of impossible odds, and louder people get more attention.

In the words of my daughter: "Not today!"

This story matters, and I hope you all know how magnifique your office in the city truly is.

I've worked with Élan Voyages for six years. What they did wasn't just good service. No. Let's not cheapen their work by calling it "good service." It was consistent, human, emotionally intelligent care.

That might be common in France.

It's not anywhere else I know.

And if you looked at my passport then you'd know I've been.

Oh, and by the way, my first passport stamp from when I was 16, can you guess where it was?

France.

Really, it's making me wonder if the French are my people.

Je suis Warren. Très bien. It's a start.

I'm especially hoping Luc might see this too. He was the first person who helped me back in 2019. He was kind, and he was genuinely excited for me to learn about Colombia. No ego. No bro attitude. Just real.

Isaline took over after that and has been helping me ever since. I'm sure she's already seen the review. But I'd like supervisors and managers, the people who make decisions about recognition, raises, awards, and promotions, to see it too.

I dropped some pictures from both adventures. Can you guess which came first?

Spoiler: the gray hair should help.

Thanks for reading. I just needed to make sure the right people know what kind of team they have in Colombia.

The right kind of team.

With all my respect and admiration,

Warren

BT dubs

(Short for "btw," short for "by the way")

Vincent Cassel has always been one of my favorite actors. I liked him in Brotherhood of the Wolf, believed in him in Derailed, and was in awe in Eastern Promises. I wasn't even sure he was French the way he lost himself in his roles.

You may notice a time gap and yes, I haven't really watched TV since I became a teacher in 2012.

But Isaline recommended My King.

I haven't watched it yet, but it's at the very top of my list.

And that should tell you something.

And if any of you ever cross paths with Mbappé — give him a fist bump for me, s'il vous plaît.

Merci,

Warren

***

The bosses needed to see the review. I had to be sure the team got their credit, recognition, and raises.

It was my fault they had a less than stellar week.

I finally found it. I hit number one. It lit up.

My stomach shifted as it lowered.

Episode VI: Return of the Traveler

Chapter F The Second Visit

The elevator door opened on the first floor. My eyes were wide. I couldn't let them shut without permission.

I went to the restaurant and got food.

Señor Ramos made me coco tea. I insisted I tip him. He said no.

I then had the front desk call the doctor again. Ramos came up to my room with a phone. He translated.

I confirmed it was only my head. They then said they would be sending a doctor. The virtual visit wasn't enough. They knew I needed hands-on care.

They said to remain in bed and not go anywhere. I said eso escucho bien.

It was perfect.

No calls. No messages. No disruptions.

I could feel where I was.

My mind and body were together.

My being was intact.

So was my soul.

And I still had my phone.

With my stories tightly in hand.

Part 35 Friends

I got comfortable on the bed. I rearranged the pillows.

An hour later the doctor and his medical partner arrived. Call him Dr. Raul Castillon. Call his partner Señora Rosalina Flores. He was more confident in English than anyone I met. He did all the basics and drew a blank.

Then Dr. Castillon looked around at my Gatorade bottles. Jinkies, he must have thought. He had a mystery to solve. Castillon looked at my tongue and said I was badly dehydrated. I said my pee was orange and smelly.

***

He put two lines and four bags of IVs in my arm. Nobody left the room until it was done: Dr. Castillon, Sra. Flores, and Sr. Ramos.

***

As he put the IV in, he talked to me about the NFL. After he was getting my height and weight, I tried to do the math from imperial to metric. He asked why does my country insist on those measures? I said I really don't know, but there is an amazing SNL sketch on that very topic. Without missing a beat, he took out his phone and pulled up the sketch. Castillon already knew it. Most Americans don't.

It's about George Washington telling his soldiers about freedom for weights and measures and how little sense it will make because "We are free men!" We laughed and laughed. I leaned back, trying to stay awake and keep my eyes from rolling into my head.

Dr. Castillon told me where he was from in Colombia. I told him the site near there I wanted to see but (Isaline) advised against. He said it is so isolated that it's more expensive than international flights, so she was right to advise against it.

I showed Castillon and Rosalina the pic from dinner and asked who I was married to. They both guessed Isaline.

I told the story of La Tienda and asked if my guide was wrong. Castillon said I absolutely had that if I wanted it. I asked what the woman said? He said who cares, the words really didn't matter. I mattered. Rosalina blushed. He told her the story, and she said sí. Dr. Castillon said in their country, I would have no problems with women, and he winked in the direction of Sra. Flores.

Then we talked about soccer, football, basketball, cricket, and hockey as they changed out my IVs.

Flores said la cabeza tiene el color. Or something like that. My face had color.

***

I told Dr. Castillon that I needed to do something for them. He said he doesn't take tips. I took a breath, and I knew this would sound arrogant. Well then, I guess I will have to make you famous, and I nodded to my phone.

I got their full names and company names so I could.

He told me he needed me to stay in bed, eat what I can tolerate, and drink Pedialyte.

W: Can I fly out tomorrow?

Dr: Yes.

W: Do I need to worry about anything?

Dr: No. Plane altitude will not make it worse but be sure you eat and drink on the plane.

W: So, the hardest part will be the process of getting to the airport and then getting to the plane.

Dr: Yes. But you've done far worse. I see the scars on your body in the exam. And I heard them in your heart.

***

Flores went to take the IV out and got nervous. She became flushed and scared. I wasn't sure why. I needed her to take out the IV and not call in Castillon. I didn't want her going home thinking she sucked at her job.

She didn't get proper Spanish from me, so you won't get it either.

Muchas gracias, señora. Gracias. Soy mejor. No tengo un problema. Yo necesito Usted ahora. No male a me.

She relaxed a bit but got scared about the tape and tearing it off my arm.

No male a me señora. Gracias.

She stared at my arm intently and wiped beads away.

I looked at Dr. Castillon with eyes saying don't rescue her. He nodded back.

I whispered no malo a me. No malo a me.

She got more confident.

No malo a me.

She did it. Flores's face was red, and she looked away.

Then she panicked because I bled.

¿Está rojo, sí? Siempre con IV.

She held pressure on it and her eyes were wide. I would not say tranquila.

Yo pienso que soy más mejor, señora.

I wonder if she just heard a delirious gringo trying to speak Spanish.

But she didn't have to call Castillon to save it. She did it. She didn't have to question herself on my account.

And really, what is an IV? *Oh no, not a little extra blood. Oh no, not a hair pulled off.* This was more. This was a young lady who doubted herself and didn't need to.

They got up to leave and asked that I get rest.

I grabbed my phone and said first, I have a review to write and a story to tell.

And we all enjoyed the moment of silence.

But I was sad that they would leave.

And I really needed support for what came next.

Part 36 The Letter

I still wasn't feeling great, but I had answers. I got on my phone to complete my job.

I wrote my letter.

To Whom It May Concern:

My name is Warren Shmith, and I stayed at the Mariton by Bogotá Airport from August 4 to August 6.

I was supposed to continue my holiday until Friday, August 8.

I was feeling ill, and when I left for Bogotá with plans to go on to Cartagena, I felt like I would fall. I decided to remain in Bogotá to get a hotel and rest up with a doctor's visit before leaving.

The Bogotá staff is special. Every person working there went above and beyond to ensure I was comfortable and cared for. Nobody treated me less than because I couldn't stand or because I lost the color in my face.

I was sick enough that I was forgetting my Spanish, and not one person made it difficult for me. They stayed with me and allowed me to keep my pride as I tried and failed their language. They gently corrected me as my brain was not accessible. Many destinations would just speak English to save time.

Not this staff. They worked with me to help me through it, even when I couldn't recall basic words I've said hundreds of thousands of times. They should be commended for respecting my dignity and demonstrating the skill I find to be the most important: emotional intelligence.

I need to thank Sr. Paulo Ramos, the manager on duty. He arrived with the medical provider since she did not know English and spoke quickly. He made sure I understood what she knew. He personally made me coco tea.

The next day he checked on me many times, both in person and by phone. He made me more coco tea. I told him I wasn't better, and another doctor arrived. Sr. Ramos stayed to ensure I was cared for. He even arranged a visit to the pharmacy so someone could get my medicine and Pedialyte.

He wouldn't accept any gratuity or gift. He insisted it's a service and his pleasure.

This man should be given promotions, raises, recognitions, and he deserves to be celebrated. People in the U.S. might do this, but it is often for the tip or because they are required to. Sr. Ramos took joy in taking care of me.

I also want you to keep your partnership with the medical company.

They weren't just doctors and medical providers. They were my rescue. At first it was thought to be something in the altitude or water.

Dr. Raul Castillon and Sra. Rosalina Flores identified the culprit instantly: I was dehydrated. They knew after one look at my tongue.

They ended up attaching two lines and four bags of IVs. All three of my rescuers stayed with me the whole time.

I hope you see how special this is. It matters. Maybe in Colombia it's the standard. But I've been around and am a world traveler. This isn't my typical, but it should be the standard.

Dr. Castillon spoke phenomenal English. He asked me about American football as he administered IVs to keep my mind occupied. We joked about how the U.S. refuses the metric system, and we watched the SNL skit where George Washington explains the silly reasoning as "freedom."

You have a thoughtful and intelligent doctor who knows how to make a patient relax. Not once was I uncomfortable or uneasy. He is another example of a human being with high emotional intelligence.

I didn't know I would talk about Peyton Manning, Joe Montana, Tom Brady, Michael Jordan, and LeBron James. I was ready to talk about Messi and Ronaldo. But he saw my NFL hat and knew how to reach me.

Do not let this doctor go. I know many doctors in the U.S. who do not care this much about a patient. Some never would talk about sports, especially sports from another country.

Sra. Flores was less confident in English, and I was so sick I wasn't available in my Spanish; however, empathy isn't a spoken language. She was there. When she removed my IVs, she was nervous because she didn't want to harm me. She sighed as she peeled tape off from my arm saying, "No."

I tried to comfort her, but it sounded like a delirious American trying Spanish.

Sra. Flores is on her way to the top. Remember that when you give her a raise or extend her contract.

When they left, I was upset. They were my amigos.

You need to know that your Bogotá location is gold, and I knew it would be this way. That's why I stopped in Bogotá.

Be sure Sr. Ramos, Dr. Castillon, and Sra. Flores are recognized and celebrated. Or promoted. Or given raises.

They would not let me show my appreciation with tips. I'm a teacher. I live in a world where doing your job well, giving your best, and recognizing the good ones are forgotten when other aspects of the job are present.

I imagine hospitality and medical professionals are similar.

On my watch, their selflessness will be recognized.

Now do your part.

Sincerely,

Warren Schmidt, MEd

They wouldn't accept my tips or gifts. I hope they will accept their places in my book.

Part 37 Night Attack

I started feeling stronger as I drank Pedialyte and balanced it with food. I was not back yet, but I was told it could take a while.

That night, my wife sent me messages about what time I needed to be awake, leave the hotel, and be at the airport.

They weren't gentle messages. She was still trying to control me.

I wrote back to let me do it my way. I've done worse. I've used that airport before. I've got this.

Quit trying to fix it your way.

***

My mom called me on a video call. She never does that. I declined.

Boomers are going to boom.

She called again. That's weird? I answered it.

She was surprised to be talking to me, but I was even more surprised to talk to her.

M: You badgered your wife, and that's not ok. And it's your fault. It is never acceptable to badger somebody.

W: Do you really want to just believe my wife's story? Also, hi, mom.

Then my food came. I said I would be back.

I called back and she asked why I was calling.

(???!!!??? WHAT !!!???!!!)

She said she never called.

(???!!!??? WHAT !!!???!!!)

Maybe you bumped something. But you called me, mom.

My mom squared her brows, and her tone connected like a right cross. More insults.

W: You need to be careful. I am in a whole other world, and right now, I'm not feeling the need to return. In fact, I could go anywhere, do anything, disappear, and be just fine. And you **KNOW** it's true. I'm a traveler. Not a tourist. And how many times have I vanished before?

(Silence)

W: The Colombian people care for me more than my family.

(Silence)

W: It's **sad** when a pro wrestler and French travel agent in Colombia reminds me who I am more than my family. And they show me my family just takes advantage of me and wants me to go along with it.

(Silence)

W: It's actually beyond tragic.

M: I talked to your wife and found out what happened. And that agent did her job.

W: I assume you mean Isaline, who wouldn't tolerate my wife's bullying and insults?

M: Well, yes, Warren. You are Isaline's client. That's smart business.

W: My wife is Isaline's client, too. Don't you dare cheapen it. You **know** it's different.

M: Your wife told me a lot.

W: Oh, I bet she told you plenty. Are you sure you just want to believe it?

M: I know it's true. I've seen you and know you.

W: Oh, do you know me, mom? Why are you defensive?

(Stopped)

W: Why are you so angry, mom?

M: I'm not angry.

W: Your eyebrows and tone shouted wrath the same way you say mine do. Tell me again you're not angry or tell me you are wrong when you say I'm angry. Both can't be true. I have some time to wait.

(Breathing)

W: Please remember the room is still spinning and I had four bags and two IV leads, and then you called to let me have it.

M: I didn't mean to call.

W: But you chewed me out without even listening to a word I said.

M: I didn't -

W: Yes, you did. And respectfully, I have never been so upset and disappointed in you.

M: Warren, I didn't mean it like -

W: Yes, you did. Hey mom, did you know I am writing a book?

M: No-no, I didn't.

W: Of course not. I never told, and I never was going to. I have all types of documentation of everything on this trip. Hundreds of pages. From my phone.

M: Oh. Ok? What does that mean?

W: It means I wrote down everything that's happened immediately after it did. **You picked the wrong horse**.

M: You were unkind, and she left.

W: Did you know when I was 16 to 23, I was groomed and abused by Pete's stepmom? I was never going to say a word, but now I don't care because you betrayed me.

(Eyes zooming side to side)

W: Yeah. She groomed, abused, manipulated, took, reshaped, and rewired me. This is what's left of me.

M: So, it was an inappropriate relationship?

W: YES. I love how the blame falls on me still when you say it.

(Looking up and down without moving her head)

W: Yeah, that happened.

M: Oh, my God.

W: Let's not talk about God right now. But where **WERE** you?

M: I think I met her once. She was younger and pretty, right?

W: **MOM. WHERE WERE YOU?**

M: Ummm. I really -

W: I went to you and told you because I couldn't get out, and you made a joke about The Graduate. You even repeated it in front of grandma, grandpa, and Aunt Shelly. **ONLY YOU LAUGHED!**

M: I really don't remember this.

W: But I do. I can tell you exactly where we were seated in the living room, the time of day, and what I was wearing. If you give me a minute or two, I can work backwards and tell you the month and the year.

M: Warren, I'm so sorry. But I do believe you.

W: Of course you do. *I don't lie*. I told dad too. He said it was weird and inappropriate.

M: And?

W: Mom, you know dad doesn't do anything more than that.

(Silence)

W: Mom, did you know I was raped in high school?

M: Oh, my God! Warren? Where is this coming from?

W: Did you know that dad knew, and he told me not to upset you? To **keep it quiet**?

M: Warren?!?

W: I've kept these locked away for 24 years and 17-22 years like a good son. The son I had to be. Deep in the vault of my heart. Imagine what I haven't told you about my wife. My wife whose side you are taking right now. She has a vault in my heart, too.

(Crying)

W: I cry, too, sometimes. It's less than I used to. But it's my life and it's been **24 years**. For you, it's been **two minutes**.

M: Warren, I am so sorry. I didn't see or help.

W: I know, but it was like 2001 or 2002, maybe 2004, mom. The years aren't clear. Young men weren't protected then. They still aren't, really.

(Silence)

W: I am not even mad at you for that. I'm mad you took my wife's story and framed me the villain without even hearing me after I had four FUCKING IVs, and two FUCKING lines in my arm!

(LOUD silence)

M: Warren, this is making me sick. I don't know if I can sleep.

W: I get it, mom. I can't always sleep, and I get sick all the time, too. But it will get better. At least, that's what the professionals told me. The ones you **made** me see. The ones who gave me medication.

M: I'm sorry I took her side.

W: Good. If you weren't, I'm not on the plane tomorrow, I don't know where I'm going, and I'm not your son. Bogota has connections all over the world.

(Gasps)

W: Hey mom, are you listening now? I've got over 400 pages written from my phone and thumb. Want some light reading? But it's not light.

M: Honey, I guess if I have to-

W: Mom, I'm not sick. You get to consent or not. **Unlike me, you get a choice**. But I think you should.

M: Ok, Warren. Yes, I will read.

W: And since dad has such bad dementia, and you can't trust your adult children under your roof to behave like adults, you will have to carry this alone. Like I did. It's your turn to **keep it quiet**.

M: I'm so -

W: Cool, mom. I will send you some chapters, and I will see you at the airport tomorrow, not my wife, yeah?

(Pause)

M: Okay.

W: Thanks, mom.

M: I love you, hon.

W: I bet you do. It's easy to love the one who takes it all for the team, isn't dramatic, and will defend abusiveness and abusers.

M: I'm sorry.

W: Save it, mom. Show it instead. Change your actions. Starting… tomorrow. Now I need some rest. I just underwent significant medical treatment.

M: Good night, son.

W: Sleep well, mom, and enjoy your reading.

(Click)

I got the best rest of my life.

I didn't even have to fall into myself.

I was at ease.

Part 38 Departure

I slept soundly. I could not even tell you about a dream.

The next day I got up at 4am and was ready to go. I left some cash at the front desk and said give it to Señor Ramos. He'd know what to do with it.

***

I got through the airport procedures. My Spanish returned to me. I only got on the wrong domestic flight line... three times? No biggie. I made it.

And it was Monday, so Isaline was back in the office. I knew she would say something. It was not Ondine on the emergency line now.

***

On the plane I wrote more reviews, more chapters, and more to the story on my phone.

***

When I landed, I had a message from Isaline.

It said, and these are direct quotes from the app that doesn't know what it is (you know the one):

From Isaline:

"Hi Warren, Isaline here. I was so sorry to hear that you got sick and that you were going back home.

I hope you will recover soon. Have a safe trip back home and thank you for the google comments.

Best,"

I wrote,

"Merci, Isaline.

I'm slowly getting better, and I just landed. Thank you again, for the logistics and beyond.

It really made a difference.

Wishing you the best with high season.

And I hope you get to New York soon.

À bientôt, peut-être."

That ending meant if we meet again. I had to come up with something that went beyond friends, maybe.

An hour later, I asked if she had a picture from dinner. Mine didn't turn out well. Also, My King is still at the top of my list.

Within two minutes she sent me her pic, saying here it is.

Two minutes.

And it was forwarded. She took it with her personal phone, not her work phone, and she sent it to me from her work phone.

Do the math. She forwarded it from her phone to her work phone and then to me.

**

I'm not sure what that means, but I do know she took it for herself.

Personal phone.

**

I later posted reviews all over the socials. I was tagged back a few times.

From her business accounts.

***

I have no idea what any of that means, though, aside from I can identify patterns.

Part 39 Pickup

Luggage pickup was delayed. My mom kept texting me cute pictures of my puppy, who is now six.

My mom was apologetic.

I said just don't leave me alone with my wife, and I'll probably let it all go.

My mom tried to fill any silences.

I said I'm always fine with silence. You don't need to make it disappear.

My mom said my wife will be on her best behavior for a while.

I said sure she will be. Until she isn't. And we don't know when she will snap.

***

Night two was the first major fight. I called my mom as a witness.

I said I wasn't going to counseling with my wife until she got her own help first. I will not walk in there, take all my accountability and ownership, try to find solutions, and be with someone who moments earlier told me she didn't want to make my sick ass dinner, and she could have been a bitch about it. I told her adults do not speak like children.

I reminded her that being an adult is when we choose not to behave like children. I said meet me where I am, and I will go.

She asked how long it would take.

I said I had no idea. There are no shortcuts or hacks. I don't know how long it will take. But until you can own your issues without blaming or deflecting, take accountability, drop your defenses, and sit in discomfort without fleeing, we are not on the same field. There are no formulas or scripts. It's a process.

She fired back, but I interrupted.

I said there is no fast talk. There is no winning or losing. I already lost long ago.

My mom asked what that meant.

Mom, if I have to explain that, then you haven't thought enough about it. You know what I mean.

My wife tried to fire again, and I said stop proving my points. You're making this too easy for me.

She reminded me she could be a bitch.

I said there are countless times where my behavior could have devolved, but I never told her. Remember the sacrifices I made for you when you had COVID when we were separated? I chose to do my part. Period.

My wife told me her policy now was no sex. Then she corrected it to a boundary.

I laughed and said it took a lot of weight off my shoulders. Also, that's a nice way to use my vocabulary. Is there anything else you want to plagiarize?

**

My mom still thought I needed to go with my wife to counseling. I asked my mom if she ever told someone she cared for that she didn't have to and could behave badly.

She looked at the ground and said no.

I said yeah, you know, neither have I.

My mom said a good therapist will see through it.

I said it's a good thing I've never seen a bad therapist and fist-bumped her.

I told my mom I need counseling first, too. I have an appointment with a trauma therapist from the former Balkan Bloc who will not be shaped by American 'culture.' If I know I need counseling, imagine how much more my wife needs without even realizing it.

My mom said you always do the work. She insisted it's the therapist's job to see the couple and name the dynamics.

I said I would hope you are right, but I'm choosing me. I'm choosing my health.

My mom said the only hope was counseling.

I said that may be true, but she has to take her work seriously first and learn to stay in it when it's tough.

***

To my wife and mom: I can't trust you two. I have to watch my own back. Nobody else in this country does.

The only other person who does that is in Colombia.

***

Say her name for me, please…

Part 40 My Last Email

The tension in the house was thick. But my mind was clearer than ever before.

I emailed Isaline for information for my travel insurance. My ask wasn't light. Her response was, of course, thorough and professional.

Of course it was.

She's Isaline.

And I know I'm Warren.

***

I

A

M

W

A

R

R

E

N

***

I don't know when I am reaching out again. I don't know what to say.

But I will.

Without any question or doubt, whether it be shadow of or reasonable.

If she is in New York, guess who is using his personal days?

If she drops her boyfriend, guess who's booking a flight to Colombia?

If neither happens, then that's quite disappointing.

I will find more people who make me feel like Warren.

It feels too good to be myself.

***

I would like to thank the French and Colombians for letting me know.

I'm enough.

***

To everyone else reading this, you are enough, too.

***

If you will excuse me, I must get to some pressing matters in the present.

I no longer need the safety of my mind.

***

Six Word Memoir

At my first teacher in-service, we had to write a six-word memoir. I thought the idea was lame, but mine won.

Life is more than six words.

Since then, I've opened most school years the same way.

By my fourth year, my new six-word memoir was:

Hated school, yet I'm a teacher.

Around my twelfth year, I updated it again.

My daughter taught me real love.

Now, in my sixteenth year, just weeks after the dinner that became the catalyst for this book, I have a new memoir. I can't share it with classes:

French guide met me in Colombia.

Instead, I told my students the safer version:

Wrote three books with rage, clarity.

But that's not the real memoir.

***

The End?

El Fin?

La Fin?

***

www.ingramcontent.com/pod-product-compliance
Lightning Source LLC
Chambersburg PA
CBHW021220130626
46554CB00004B/1292